Bow
Eastern Ontario

Quarry Press Cultural & Historical Companions

Finnigan's Guide to the Ottawa Valley:
A Cultural & Historical Companion
by Joan Finnigan

Brado's Guide to Ottawa:
A Cultural & Historical Companion
by Edward Brado

BOWERING'S GUIDE TO EASTERN ONTARIO
A Cultural & Historical Companion

edited by Ian Bowering

compiled by Tri-County Writers' Guild
        Eileen Cunningham
        Glenda Eden
        Patricia H. MacKenna
        Emily Madsen
        Rosemary Rutley

Quarry Press

Copyright © Quarry Press, 1992.

All rights reserved.

The publisher acknowledges the assistance of the Ontario Arts Council and The Canada Council in the production of this book.

Canadian Cataloguing in Publication Data

Bowering, Ian, 1951-
  Bowering's guide to Eastern Ontario: a cultural and historical companion.

Includes bibliographical references and index.
ISBN 1-55082-051-6

  1. Stormont, Dundas and Glengarry (Ont.) — History. 2. Stormont, Dundas and Glengarry (Ont.) — Guidebooks. I. Title. II. Title: Guide to Eastern Ontario.

FC3095.S77B69 1992   971.3'75   C92-090451-3
F1059.S89B89 1992

Cover photo by Ian Bowering. Back cover illustration by Lor Pelton.
Designed by Keith Abraham.
Printed and bound in Canada by Best-Gagné, Toronto, Ontario.

Published by Quarry Press Inc., P.O. Box 1061, Kingston, Ontario K7L 4Y5.

CONTENTS

12 Introduction

29 Chapter 1: The Perch Route
67 Chapter 2: The Fur Trade Route
109 Chapter 3: Glengarry Highland Roads
147 Chapter 4: Touring Cornwall
187 Chapter 5: The Loyalist Front Route
223 Chapter 6: The Lost Villages Adventure
271 Chapter 7: The Apple-Cheddar Route

307 Armchair Traveling:
A Guide to Further Reading
314 Local Historical Societies
and Heritage Groups
316 Travel and Tourist Information Centers
317 Index of Place Names

Preface

This book is the result of the collaborative efforts of the Tri-County Writers' Guild and myself. When I moved to Cornwall more than a dozen years ago to assume the position of curator of Inverarden Regency Cottage Museum, my knowledge of the region was academic. I knew that it was one of the earliest settled parts of the province, that much of Ontario's present day educational system was created here, but little else. Over the years as curator, Cornwall Bicentennial Coordinator, and now local history enthusiast, I started to acquire a local photographic archives. Over time I grew to understand and appreciate the region's history and traditions not related in the standard textbooks. This work attempts to bridge some of the gap between tradition and 'fact'. The book does not presume to be a comprehensive history or guide to the United Counties of Stormont, Dundas, and Glengarry; rather it is a primer to the material, culture, and heritage waiting to be discovered in the course of seven day trips that I hope will stimulate your

PREFACE

curiosity. There is much more to discover in this historically and culturally rich region of Ontario.

In producing this work I have had the pleasure of being assisted by the optimism and skills of the Tri-County Writers' Guild. It has only been with the overwhelming generosity of spirit and cooperation freely given by the authors Eileen Cunningham, Glenda Eden, Pat MacKenna, Emily Madsen, and Rosemary Rutley that this book has been completed. They in turn relied upon several colleagues for assistance. Pat MacKenna extends her most sincere thanks for their assistance to Joan Johnston, Evelyn Theakston van Beek, William and Norma Cattanach, Michael and Joan Caron, Theresa Quinn, David Anderson and Brother Joseph Vallancourt. Rosemary Rutley extends her thanks for all their assistance to Jean-Paul Bernier (Canal Co-ordinator, St. Lawrence Seaway), Ambert Brown and Frank Sisty of Iroquois, Clarence Cross of Chesterville, and Bryce Rupert of Lunenburg. Glenda Eden extends her most sincere thanks to Archie Eastman and Fran Laflamme.

In the end, all would have come to naught if Bob Hilderley and the staff at Quarry Press had not backed this project to the fullest.

IAN BOWERING

A Guide to Bowering's Guide to Eastern Ontario

Cornwall, the county seat for the United Counties of Stormont, Dundas and Glengarry, is the hub at which the seven tours in this book either originate or terminate. Travelers from Montreal or Ottawa or Kingston or New York State can easily connect with these tours, either coming to or going from Cornwall. Just read the "Directions" at the beginning and the end of each chapter or tour in order to orient yourself.

Three of the tours—"The Perch Route" (Chapter 1), "The Fur Trade Route" (Chapter 2), and "Glengarry Highland Roads" (Chapter 3)—are set in Glengarry County. Since these three tours sometimes criss-cross and overlap, you may want to read all three chapters in advance of your day (or weekend) trips. Another three tours—"The Loyalist Front Route" (Chapter 5), "The Lost Villages Adventure" (Chapter 6), and "The Apple-Cheddar Route"

A GUIDE TO BOWERING'S GUIDE

(Chapter 7)—are set in Stormont and Dundas Counties. These three tours also criss-cross and overlap, making them ideal for a long weekend adventure. The central chapter is devoted to a tour of Cornwall, the Seaway capital of Eastern Ontario.

Before venturing forth on these tours, be sure to pick up good maps of the region, available in person or by mail from the tourism and travel agencies listed in an appendix near the end of this guide. But don't worry about getting lost in Eastern Ontario—you may discover much more than can be found in these pages, including extremely hospitable people and lots of perch, cheddar cheese, and apples to sustain you until you find your way home again.

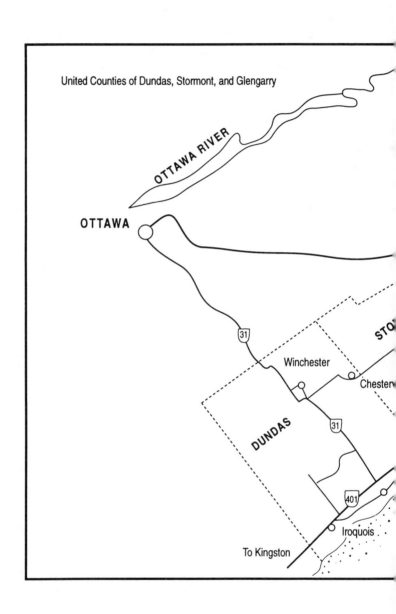

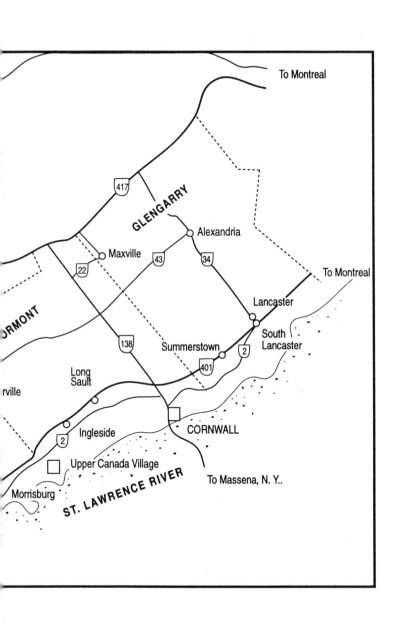

Introduction

The old bromide that we'll travel 1,000 kilometers to visit a museum, but not take time to learn what's in our own backyard is often true. When publisher Bob Hilderley called me several years ago with the idea of writing a book about my own backyard, my initial response was, "It can't be done."

Thinking about it that night I realized I'd made a tremendous mistake. What I meant to say was that the project couldn't be done by one person. The next morning I called Bob and said I'd like to do the project as a joint effort with the Tri-County Writers' Guild. I said that six people would be able to explore the region thoroughly and present fresh approaches to each topic.

That night I telephoned the prospective authors to sell the idea to them. They were enthusiastic. So I sketched out seven routes crossing Eastern Ontario, we met, selected our interests, and set out on our quest to discover Stormont, Dundas, and Glengarry. But first we have to correct a few misconceptions about our region...

INTRODUCTION

In 1984 the City of Cornwall and the United Counties of Stormont, Dundas, and Glengarry prepared to celebrate the Bicentennial of the arrival of the United Empire Loyalists. I was hired as Cornwall's Bicentennial Coordinator to mark this event with a year-long series of celebrations. For five years the City, prodded by Miss Jean Cameron and Stanley McNairn of the Stormont, Dundas, and Glengarry Historical Society had been planning these events; we had even commissioned Dr. Elinor Kyte Sr. to write a history to mark the occasion.

Regally ensconced in my Pitt Street office with a staff of three and a volunteer management committee of ten, I received a somewhat surprising letter from the Ontario Bicentennial Advisory Commission, formed to celebrate the bicentennial of the founding of the province, advising us that we should be organizing events to celebrate the 150th anniversary of Cornwall. What did the politicians and historical gurus in Toronto know that we didn't?

It's a belief firmly held by the citizens of Eastern Ontario that the provincial government (it doesn't matter what party holds power) seems to think Ontario's eastern border ends somewhere between Kingston and Morrisburg. In many ways we at the eastern end of the province prefer this situation; although government interest provides funds in the short run, in the long term such assistance always ends up costing something. This time government intervention heralded a new history—a slight problem considering we already had a history.

After a few telephone calls and letters I was able to give the bureaucrats in Toronto the correct version of our heritage and let them know that we didn't need the second date at all, as we were quite happy with the one we had. It turned out that the Bicentennial Advisory Commission had selected 1834 because that was the date Cornwall was officially incorporated as a town. At that time it had a population of 1,000 and was managed by an elected Board of Police which consisted of four men chosen from the town's two wards, who in turn selected a fifth member as chairman or president. Only to an historian of municipal politics could this date have had any significance—or perhaps they had heard that Monday night council meetings, made possible by this incorporation, held well over a century later, and broadcast over the local cable TV channel, had become the most popular show in town.

However the error arose, it made me think about the whole issue of historic dates and question Cornwall's founding date of 1784. Hadn't the French given the navigational point on the St. Lawrence near present-day Cornwall the name Pointe Maligne (Cape Fear) long before then? And what about the Native settlement at St. Regis?

Research quickly demonstrated that the date Cornwall was first settled (and for that matter Eastern Ontario) is a matter of historical debate. The Loyalists proudly and justifiably claim to have founded present-day Ontario. Not wishing to remain in the United States after the Treaty of Versailles granted the 13 Colonies independence in 1783, many of the former colonials who had remained loyal to Britain by fighting the rebels decided to take the Imperial Government's offer of free land, and they came to Canada.

Numbering around 10,000 people, the Loyalists followed two routes into Canada. One group settled in the Maritimes and Quebec. Another group settled along the Niagara Frontier, and from the Bay of Quinte east to the present Quebec border. Settlement was not immediate since much of present day Ontario belonged to the Natives in the traditional sense and had been reserved for them by the British. According to Gerald Craig in *Upper Canada: The Formative Years*, the Governor of Quebec, General Frederick Haldimand, originally believed that "...the refugees of European origin" should be settled in the Maritimes and that present day Ontario "should be reserved to the Indians, whose loyalty to Britain was being sorely tried by reports of the peace treaty with the United States."

To counteract the Natives' sense of betrayal, Haldimand sent Surveyor General Major Samuel Holland west in the spring of 1783 to survey land for Native settlement. Holland's reports regarding the advantages of the St. Lawrence Valley, the growing need to find a home for the Loyalists, and the fact that the Natives "would not regard the Loyalists as unwelcome invaders" but as "old comrades-in-arms" persuaded Haldimand to begin planning the settlement of present day Ontario.

The land, however, was not the Crown's to give away. In Eastern Ontario, the Mohawks living at St. Regis, a reserve created in the 1750s under the protective and religious guidance of the Jesuits, believed that they had claim to both banks of the St. Lawrence and the river's islands, for hunting if not for settlement. This claim was reinforced by the Royal Proclamation of 1763 which, along with the creation of civilian government for British North America, drew the boundaries of Quebec. To the south the province ended roughly along the west bank of rivers flowing into the Atlantic, closely approximating the present day Ontario-Quebec border.

Hilda Neatby in *Quebec 1760-1791: The Revolutionary Age* goes on to state that the Proclamation officially recognized Natives as 'Nations' or 'Tribes' under British protection and as "subjects of the King." This was done in order to pacify the Natives after the Pontiac uprising. Having guaranteed ownership of the north shores of the Great Lakes and St. Lawrence to the Native peoples, Imperial policy then protected it by forbidding private purchases of land from them. Only the Crown could acquire it through formal treaties with individual tribes.

The Loyalists, who were living in camps, felt Haldimand was not moving quickly enough. To appease his men, Lieutenant-Colonel Sir John Johnson of the King's Royal Regiment of New York ordered Patrick McNiff to make a quick survey of Eastern Ontario. On these instructions McNiff and his men divided the land into nine Royal Townships, starting east of the seigniory of Longueuil hugging the north bank of the St. Lawrence to the Thousand Islands.

While making preparations for the incoming Loyalists, Johnson visited Pointe Maligne, the future location of Cornwall, to be met by "a great number

INTRODUCTION

of the Chiefs and Warriors" who "thought it would be unjust... to take away from them... the lands they had always looked upon as theirs." Elinor Senior, in her history of Cornwall, goes on to state that they claimed the north shore of the St. Lawrence from the Raisin River in Lancaster to the Long Sault Rapids. This issue immediately stopped McNiff and his men from surveying any further and sent Sir John Johnson back to Montreal to confer with Governor Haldimand about their next move.

After reviewing the register of Crown lands to verify the Natives' claim, Haldimand discovered that there was no record of any grant. According to Senior:

> As the Indians had no "legal right to the lands"... but had been taught "to consider them as their property and have been in the custom of reaping advantages from them..." he urged that it would not be "political or right to contend the point with them provided they are satisfied with reasonable terms."

At this point the Mohawk Chief, Captain Joseph Brant, offered to intervene on behalf of his kinsman Sir John Johnson and his men. In early May 1784 Brant secured for the British the north shore of the river with the exception of a tract of land almost three miles wide running from the St. Lawrence to the Nation River between the First and Second Townships, while the Indians kept Grand Isle (now Cornwall Island) and Petite Isle.

The way now clear, Johnson led the men of the First Battalion King's Royal Regiment of New York, and a contingent of the Royal Highland Emigrants (84th), to the British army depot at the future site of Cornwall sometime around 6 June 1784.

Originally named New Johnstown to honor their leader, Township 2 (later Cornwall) was reported to have a population of 215 men, 87 women, and 214 children by October. Throughout Eastern Ontario the disbanded troops were resettled, according to the wishes of the British authorities and their own leaders, in communities that included their former religious, ethnic, and military brothers. For this reason, the Catholic Highlanders were granted land in Eastern Glengarry, the Scottish Presbyterians settled next to them, the Germans were next, and finally the Anglicans took up residence in Dundas County. Within a month Sir John reported that 1,568 men, 626 women, 1,492 children, and 90 servants had settled in the first of the five Royal Townships.

This reconciles with the claim that the Eastern Townships were settled in 1784. The Natives were present previous to this date but did not occupy the land directly. But what about the French?

It appears that although the French fur traders and explorers traveled through this section of Eastern Ontario, and lumbermen from Montreal paid the Indians at St. Regis to cut their timber, Pointe Maligne was a navigational point on the map, and not a settlement. This fact is reinforced by evidence that even the English bargemen who towed the bateaux in front of the town referred to the rapids by the French name until the 1830s.

The histories of the small communities along the riverfront follow two patterns of development. The riverfront from Lancaster to Cornwall differs markedly from the "Front" west of Cornwall because, although the entire region was settled by Loyalists, only Lancaster developed a manufacturing base. Other industrial towns failed to materialize in southern Glengarry because no canals were dug, which would have provided the necessary waterpower. Without a source of automotive power, the Glengarry Front remained largely rural, eventually attracting tourists for its fishing and scenery at the turn of the century.

In the absence of development, the Glengarry Front has maintained a direct link with its Loyalist heritage and retains its rural character, unlike the Front of Stormont and Dundas Counties which was served by canals, industrialized, and then permanently obliterated by the construction of the St. Lawrence Seaway.

So, that clears up some historical misconceptions and introduces some geographical directions. But what about the way outsiders mistake the character of the people who live in Eastern Ontario? I'm not from Stormont, Dundas, or Glengarry; as a local historian this distance permits me to view the region objectively. Like many newcomers transplanted here from large urban centers like Ottawa or Toronto, I laughed at the five minute traffic jams, but soon came to enjoy the fact that I had more free time, occasioned by the fact that I didn't spend an hour or more commuting.

I found it quaint that guards had to posted on the new escalators at Cornwall Square Shopping Centre since many people had never ridden on such contraptions, even in 1980. I also scoffed at the term "use guys," heard so often throughout the area that it separates locals from outsiders.

I have not been alone in having unflattering first impressions of Stormont, Dundas, and Glengarry. Almost from the outset the United Counties have received bad press. Witness the following.

Government Surveyor Patrick McNiff, while acknowledging that the land some distance north of the St. Lawrence was good, wrote that the Lancaster Front was generally low and wet, and not "fit for Culture" unless drained. Furthermore, all of the best timber had been cut, and there was only one location suitable for a mill, at the mouth of the Raisin River.

Charlottenburgh Township fared little better in McNiff's estimation. He noted that the land along the Front was "high, Rich and Dry," but becomes stony further inland, and that there was no valuable timber left, or stream constant enough to power a mill.

Township No. 2, which became Cornwall, while largely denuded of trees provided "...two places very convenient for erecting mills on" and was also "high, Rich and Dry." It is no wonder Cornwall became the favored choice of the Loyalists, as McNiff went on to describe Osnabruck Township to the west as having "very indifferent—stony or sandy" land.

INTRODUCTION

Canada Steamship Lines Steamer "Rapids Queen" shooting the Long Sault Rapids c. 1920. Courtesy Stormont, Dundas & Glengarry Historical Society, Inverarden Museum.

After spending a night "at Coll. Gray's, at Gray's Creek," Lieutenant-Governor Simcoe's wife Elizabeth wrote in her diary on 26 June 1792:

> As it would be very tedious to go up the Long Sault in the boat, we propose riding beyond that and another rapid called Galettes. We set off about ten o'clock. On our way we passed through Cornwall...a settlement four miles from Coll. Gray's. There are about fifteen houses and some neat gardens in them; and rode eleven miles to Mr. Macdonell's at the Long Sault, his farm being very near that Grand Rapid, which continues a mile; the whole of the river foaming like white breakers, and the banks covered with thick woods, is a very fine sight.

Lieutenant Francis Hall of the 14th Light Dragoons was the next visitor to leave a written account in his book printed in 1818 titled *Travels in Canada, and The United States, 1816 and 1817*. Frustratingly, he just gives us the smallest glimpse:

> 'Tis a sad waste of life to ascend the St. Lawrence in a bateau. After admiring the exertions with which the Canadian boatmen, who seem to have exclusive possession of this employment, force their long flat-bottomed barks against the rapids, there is nothing left but to gaze listlessly

on the descending current, and its low wooded shores; while the monotony of the oarstroke is scarcely broken by the occasional rustling of a wild duck through the sedge, or cry of the American King-fisher, as he darts from some hanging bough on his scaly prey. It cost us 15 hours to row from Coteau-du-Lac to Cornwall, with but one incident during the voyage; this was a purchase, or rather barter, of biscuit for dried eels, with a party of half-naked Indians, whom we found idly occupied, under a clump of trees on the shore, in curing the produce of their fishery. Several of their birch canoes were anchored among the islands, or glancing along the stream, as we passed the neighbourhood of St. Regis... A stage-waggon runs from Montreal to Prescott, and carries the mail, which is afterwards conveyed on horseback to Kingston; I took it at Cornwall, and can answer for its being one of the roughest conveyances on either side of the Atlantic.

In 1821 English traveler John Howison, Esq. wrote *Sketches of Upper Canada* after a sojourn of two and a half years. Professing to promote Upper Canada Howison was less than kind when he visited Glengarry:

> I shall now introduce you to the Upper Province, and for the present dismiss the polished and interesting peasantry of Lower Canada, that I may make you acquainted with the blunt and uncultivated inhabitants of Glengarry...

The account becomes less flattering as he continues. Fortunately, Howison bypassed Cornwall on his way to Prescott only noting after leaving Glengarry that there was nothing remarkable or noteworthy there.

The Reverend Thomas Radcliffe in his *Authentic Letters from Upper Canada* published in Dublin in 1883 praised "the exquisite beauty" of the river scenery but was not pleased with Cornwall:

> The hotel at Cornwall is a wretched place, bad attendance, worse rooms, ill furnished; —vile beds, and no rest;—not a very good preparation for a long days journey... commenced, however, before five o'clock, with a great delight at quitting our uncomfortable stations... Our carriages were drawn by four horses each, and very briskly, notwithstanding the heaviness of the roads... The road here was merely a green field, stripped of its grassy surface, but up by various ruts and mud holes, and crossed by swamps and hollow channels, impassable, except by means of loose planks and timbers, which hopped and bounded under the wheels, without the security of rail or battlement, making the least nervous of

INTRODUCTION

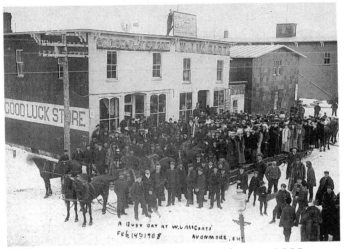

**A busy day in Avonmore, 14 February 1908.
Photo courtesy S. D. & G. Historical Society.**

the party glad to close their eyes and 'curtains', against the danger.

In 1851 W.H. Smith in his two volume set *Canada, Past, Present and Future* became a master of the back-handed compliment. He refers to Alexandria as "a busy little place," and states that Lancaster "is well watered, well settled, and contains numerous good farms." Cornwall, according to Smith, was:

> ...a neat, quiet, pleasant, old-fashioned looking place...The streets are regularly laid out, running upwards from the river, with others crossing at right angles; and there are several good houses scattered through the town.

But he continues:

> Cornwall is not a place of any great business. Cornwall remains rather stationary. In 1845 its population was stated at about 1,600; but in 1850, the number of inhabitants, according to the census, only amounted to 1,506.

As Smith progresses downriver he eventually finds "a perfect village" at Charlesville, which despite its perfection possessed a number of buildings "...of a second-rate character."

Morrisburg received the first truly favorable

report when the *Canadian Illustrated News* for 2 March 1878 reported:

> The first impression a person receives on entering Morrisburg is that he is among well-to-do people. Everywhere are to be seen residences, which would grace the streets of any of our cities, and, in the business quarter, there are blocks and buildings equally creditable.

The most slanderous image of Cornwall was painted not by an outsider, but by the editor of *The Freeholder* in an effort to belittle political opponent and M.P. Dr. Darby Bergin. Editor Alexander McLean, in his article "What Cornwall Has," listed:

> An 8¢ store, a dollar paper, a debating society, first-class hotels, any quantity of old bachelors, a junior judge, the most peculiar Council that ever graced the Chamber, a lockgate contractor, more trotting horses to the acre than any town in Canada, several financially-embarrassed merchants, the meanest man in Canada, the laziest man in America, and the biggest sneak in the universe.

This image was counteracted by *The Globe* in 1893 when they reported that Cornwall was now Canada's leading "Factory Town where ... the spirit of fairness, liberality, and honourable" business dealings were the rule.

I have come to learn that initial reactions are not always accurate. As you will find in these pages, there is much that is picturesque, unique, and fascinating in Ontario's three eastern counties. Having said this much, and—I hope—having whetted your appetite, I now deliver you into the capable hands of the members of the Tri-County Writers' Guild. They will reveal Stormont, Dundas, and Glengarry to you—where the province began.

Ian Bowering
Inverarden, Ontario

CHAPTER 1

The Perch Route

Preamble

Once thought uninhabitable by officialdom because of their swampy nature, Glengarry's Sunken Townships, starting at the Quebec border and following the riverfront west almost to Cornwall, have proven to be a paradise for wildlife and sportsmen alike, while providing homes for early settlers and subsequent immigrants since 1784. Starting at the eastern end of the United Counties in Lancaster and crossing Highway 401 to the south side into independent-minded South Lancaster, this area provides a smorgasbord of craft and specialty shops, along with a rich heritage signified by one of Eastern Ontario's first 'make-work' projects, the Lancaster Cairn, at the mouth of the Raisin River in Lake St. Francis.

Home to gold prospector 'Cariboo' Cameron, Colonel J. MacDonell of Stonehouse Point, and fur traders John McDonald of Garth and John Duncan

Campbell (the Lairds of Inverarden), the Front's history is represented in the Lairds' estate, now Inverarden Regency Cottage Museum, on the eastern edge of Cornwall. True to their name, the Sunken Townships offer far more than man-made heritage; they are also perfect haunts for naturalists who can wander the boardwalks at the Cooper's Marsh or for anglers who want to try their luck at the numerous fishing holes.

And if you are hungry there is the famous "Lancaster Perch Roll."

We invite you to sit back and read about the numerous discoveries that await you as you start your pilgrimage through historic Stormont, Dundas, and Glengarry, where Ontario began!

I.B.

Directions

This tour begins in Lancaster, 28 kilometers east of Cornwall. Take Highway 401 to the exit for Highway 34, then turn north. You'll find yourself in the town of Lancaster, named after the English county of the same name, and bisected by Charlottenburg Township and Lancaster Township. The tour follows historic Highway 2 west to Cornwall.

THE PERCH ROUTE

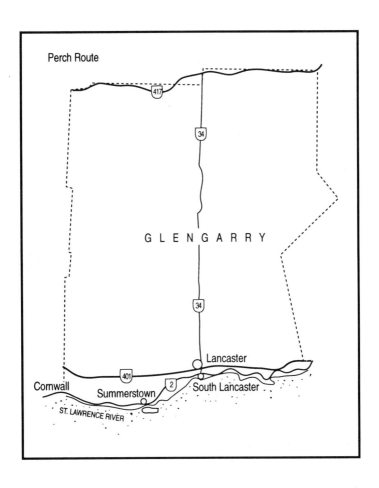

History

This region is the first "free" land the United Empire Loyalists encountered in 1784 when they arrived in what is now Eastern Ontario, and was dubbed the "Lake" or "Sunken" townships since the land was considered too swampy to be habitable. It was not generally settled by Loyalist Land Grant; however, Surveyor Lieutenant Walter Sutherland and his men found it to their liking and settled here. By October of 1784 a report of Disbanded Troops and Loyalists stated that the township had 36 men, 15 women, and 39 children. According to local historian Ewan Ross who wrote in his introduction to *Lancaster Township and Village,* "They did not belong to the first Battalion King's Royal Regiment of N.Y. but appear to have come in its wake expecting to be granted land along with them."

One of these pioneers was William Falkner (or Faulkner) who is believed to have erected the township's first house in present day South Lancaster. In his honor, the settlement was named Faulkner until 1789. Still not fully surveyed in 1785, the arrival of the Reverend Alexander MacDonell's Highlanders from Knoydart, Scotland spurred the completion of the work. A list of the town's first residents—the McMillans, McDonalds, MacDonells, McLennans, MacDongalds, and McKays—gives evidence of the area's strong Scots roots.

As if to prove the government surveyors wrong, this land fronted by the St. Lawrence River proved to be very habitable. Indeed, in another twist of fate this region—starting at the Quebec border on the east and running to Gray's Creek on the west, with the exception of Cornwall—is all that remains of the historic Loyalist waterfront. The more suitable land to the west was flooded to make way for the St. Lawrence Seaway.

Lancaster

The town of Lancaster grew along the waterfront where William MacIntosh operated a store and constructed a wharf to ship local timber and potash by bateaux. With this wharf, the village became known as the "Gateway to Glengarry." The town's waterfront location permitted easy access for new settlers and a convenient outlet for hinterland products.

During the first half of the nineteenth century the settlement was variously known as Rivière Raisin, Kirktown, Lower Village, and finally South Lancaster. In 1855 the Grand Trunk Railway opened a station a little more than a kilometer north of the Raisin River and the village was divided. According to Ewan Ross, the Lancaster station was also known as Lancaster Depot, The Upper Village, and New Lancaster. It became the commercial center while South Lancaster evolved as the residential district. The first run of what came to be known as "The Moccasin Train" took place on 19 November 1855; its last run was 103 years later, on 8 August 1958. The period from 1855 to 1882, when the Canada-Atlantic Railway arrived in Alexandria, was Lancaster's "Golden Age." The town had three warehouses and

**Fraser House, Main Street, Lancaster.
Photo by Pat MacKenna.**

two freight sheds, and was served by as many as ten passenger trains daily. Farmers and entrepreneurs came from all over the country, drawn by the bustle and commerce.

After 1958 Lancaster's population began to decline; in 1976 the town had only 500 inhabitants. The political situation in Quebec after 1976 reversed the trend and the population grew by 50%, to 750.

Today Lancaster offers a small community lifestyle with excellent access to the east, west, and north, and all the recreational advantages of the Raisin River and the St. Lawrence close by. Tourist trade is brisk on the main street, Military Road (Highway 34). There are craft and specialty shops, restaurants and excellent bed and breakfasts. Wander along main street and visit the shops featuring antiques and collectibles. The charming staircase in Fraser House has doorstops sitting on every step, each with an individual character to ponder over.

Enter the cool, tastefully decorated Browse Around Tea Room and fortify yourself with a specialty tea or coffee and a light lunch. Sample beautifully presented salads or sandwiches, or sip delicious homemade soups such as Beef and Barley. Desserts are irresistible, made fresh daily from fruit in season or luscious chocolate. On a hot summer day, a long cool glass of iced tea perfumed with lemon hits the spot. Before leaving, go upstairs to examine the crafts and other treasures. In the Christmas Room, trees are decorated with ornaments from Europe and the Orient, and have rocking horses and other nostalgic toys spread beneath them. Buy a Christmas

Auld Kirktown Craft and Gift Shoppe, South Lancaster. A 19th century fanning mill manufactured by Young Brothers of Almonte is to the right of the entrance. Photo by Pat MacKenna.

decoration to tuck away until the festive holiday. It will remind you of your outing.

A short drive south over Highway 401 there is a veritable doll house of treasures perched on a small hill. It is the Auld Kirktown Craft and Gift Shoppe created by Madeline and her husband Ranald McDonald, from Scotland. In a delightful blending of cultures, and with a discriminating eye for quality, they have made it a pleasurable place to visit. The scent of potpourri greets you at the door. Some of the items offered for sale are hand-crafted by local artisans, while others come from as far afield as Prince Edward Island, Nova Scotia, and British Columbia. It is a fairyland at Christmas, and they have a Christmas room all year round for those who like to plan ahead. Outside the front door there is an item that piques curiosity. It is a fanning mill manufactured by Young Bros. of Almonte, Ontario in the 1800s and used in that area.

Near the Lancaster exit from Highway 401, on the South Service Road, there is an attractive village square centered around Rob MacIntosh giftshops combining new buildings and old moved here from other areas. The old Bank of Montreal building, transported from Williamstown, restored and filled with collectibles, is a remnant from the days before more sophisticated banking procedures. The floor has been reinforced to accommodate the weight of a massive iron safe made by the J.H. Taylor Safe Works Company of Toronto, established 1855. From this building you can browse your way through a connecting gallery to a school house which opened 15 August 1898 in School Section #2, Locheil. A document on the wall attests to some surprising prices: the original cost to build the school was $550.00, the furnace was $64.00, grading the yard was $35.00, and putting up a fence $13.00!

South Lancaster

For a change of pace, stroll through South Lancaster. Hidden from the bustle of Highway 34, next to South Lancaster's attractive limestone Presbyterian Church on Church Street, nestles the Glengarry Tole Art Studio. Universal in its origins, tole art is a decorative form in which certain basic elements never change. Traditional forms and colors link together the decorative arts of many nations.

Janice Montreuil, resident artist, says, "If it's not tied down, it gets painted on." Some of her most unconventional materials have become her best projects! Her studio is filled with brightly-colored tin ware and wooden objects. On her door a gaily painted perch marking Lancaster's 1984 bicentennial welcomes you.

The historic Presbyterian Church next to the studio was built in 1787. Here you can walk along peaceful lanes named Knox, Calvin, and Bethune. Near the waterfront is a small cemetery with a waist-high stone wall and a plaque reading:

> Faulkner's Settlement 1784-1984. At this site United Empire Loyalists landed and formed a settlement in honor of Wm.

Janice Montreuil's Glengarry Tole Art Sudio, South Lancaster. "Tole" is Dutch for tin.
Photo by Emily Madsen.

Faulkner J.P., an area representative for Sir John Johnson. Many early settlers are buried here.

Tall trees mute sounds from the highway, and the waters of Lake St. Francis lapping the shoreline create a serene atmosphere. Take the opportunity to walk quietly among the gravestones, some of them worn faceless by the elements, and consider that you are not in an ending place, but a small corner of Canada's beginning.

A short walk west farther along Church Street and south on King Street will take you to the Lancaster Pier, now a mecca for fishermen. From there you can see the Lancaster Cairn on Monument Island. Local tradition relates that the Cairn is situated on Squaw Island, but navigational maps locate Squaw Island several kilometers to the west of the monument. Located at the mouth of the Raisin River, the Cairn is technically in Charlottenburg Township. The plaque placed on the monument in 1905 states:

> This Cairn was erected under the supervision of Lt. Colonel Lewis Carmichael of the Imperial Army, then stationed in this district on particular service by the Highland Militia of Glengarry which has aided in the suppression of the Canadian Rebellion of 1837-38. To commemorate the services of that distinguished soldier, Sir John Colborne, who was declared by the historian Sir Charles Napier to have been 'a man with a singular talent for

**The Falkland Graveyard in South Lancaster is the final resting place for the Township's first pioneers.
Photo by Pat MacKenna.**

war' and who commanded her Majesty's Forces in Canada at that critical period. He had previously served with conspicuous merit throughout the Peninsular War and elsewhere and had particularly distinguished himself at Waterloo when in command of the 52nd Regiment. He was Lieutenant Governor of Upper Canada from November 1828-January 1836, Governor General of Canada in 1839 and afterward become Field Marshall Lord Seaton G.C.B.

The Cairn, made of fieldstone with a mortared exterior, has a circumference slightly larger than 43 meters, a 63 step spiral staircase approximately 15 meters high. It is surmounted by a Napoleonic vintage 1.25 meter cannon.

That is the official history of the Cairn. While it was ostensibly built to honor Sir John Colborne, it was really a make-work project to keep idle militiamen quartered in Lancaster out of harm's way. Some 1,200 Glengarry Militiamen in two regiments under the commands of Colonel Donald McDonell of Lancaster and Lieutenant Colonel Alexander Fraser of Williamstown had been called out twice in 1838 to resist rebels in Lower and Upper Canada. Rather than disperse the men after the second tour of duty, Lieutenant Colonel Carmichael decided to quarter the men in Lancaster over the winter. Knowing the Highlanders' reputation for zeal and lack of discipline, Carmichael offered two alternatives. They could either march back and forth to Williamstown

A picnic on Monument Island in front of the Glengarry Cairn while workers reface the stone surface. Circa 1959. Photo courtesy Stormont, Dundas & Glengarry Historical Society, Inverarden Museum (91-15.6).

every day, or build the Cairn. The inexact proportions of the final product suggest that they chose building the Cairn as the lesser of two evils. Tradition holds that the project failed to keep the men away from the opposite sex, as the women were said to have helped carry the stones over the ice in their aprons. When completed, it was dedicated, around 1840, to Sir John with a "Royal Highland banquet and whisky galore." The Cairn is now under the jurisdiction of Canada's National Park Service and the island is used for picnics.

The first steamboats started navigating Lake St. Francis between the rapids at Coteau and the rapids above Cornwall in 1826. Two years later the *Neptune*, a sidewheeler tug, began calling in at Lancaster. The Moose Head Inn on the Old Montreal Road was built in 1826, no doubt to meet the needs of the new traveling public. Owned by Kenny Kaye, Wright, and the Hunters, to name a few of its proprietors, this hostelry was not known as the Moose Head until the early years of the 20th century when Duncan MacPherson mounted a moose head over the front entrance. An invoice from between the two World Wars indicates that room and board was $5.00 a day and $30.00 weekly. The inn closed in the mid 1970s. Plans were made to turn it into a tea room but health regulations made the cost prohibitive. It is now a private residence.

E.C.

Fishing

Pioneers in the Lake Township looked to the waters of Lake St. Francis and the St. Lawrence River for food in those early years. From the tiny perch to fighting giants like the muskie, the quality and quantity of fish astounded them. Today local enthusiasts fish the year round. Ice fishing huts dot the bays and inlets in winter, while anglers fish from shore and boats from early spring to late fall.

In this area, fishing is in the blood, and youngsters learn from old timers how to navigate these waters. Crappies, perch, and pike swim in abundance in the weed beds and, after spawning in rivers like the Raisin, walleye or pickerel are the spring fisherman's preferred catch. There is more great walleye fishing in the fall when fish, some weighing over ten pounds, can be hooked. In the heat of summer anglers appreciate the healthy population of bass and the fearless go after muskies that can exceed 50 pounds in weight! Each summer local papers feature stories of fantastic catches, including hard-to-believe photos of proud anglers with their trophy fish.

Unaccompanied by pictures are wonderful fish stories told along the shore in pubs and cottages by "River Rats" who have spent years on the water. This one was told at a Fish Fry one hot July evening while sitting around the fire washing down the feast with some fine whisky.

This Victorian gentleman fisherman posed proudly with his catch in Thomas Lafleur's Cornwall photography studio. In 1901 a reporter noted: "the fishing grounds in the neighborhood are famous . . . . Almost every day large catches of muskellunge, black bass (and) dore are caught." Photo courtesy of the S. D. & G. Historical Society, Inverarden Museum (90-35.6).

Story

A local River Rat used to take a strong bottle with him when he went fishing. He said it was to keep out the damp and to wet his whistle on occasion. Each time he cast his line, he would take a good slug from his bottle. One day, when he had cast and slugged a good long while without a bite, he sprinkled a little on his bait and hook just for good luck. He'd barely cast off when he felt a heavy pull on his line. Instantly sober, he engaged in battle, playing his fish slowly and carefully for some few minutes. At last he hauled it into the boat and to his great surprise, the worm had the fish by the throat!

E.M.

Cooper Marsh Conservation Area

To reach the next stop on this tour, take Highway 2 (Old Montreal Road) west from Lancaster 3.3 kilometers to the Cooper Marsh Conservation Area.

You don't often get an open invitation to someone's home nor would good manners permit you to take advantage of such an offer but the Cooper Marsh Conservation Area is the exception. Twelve months of the year, seven days a week, bird-watchers, naturalists, and ordinary folk interested in wetland species may observe the nesting and feeding areas of rare and not-so-rare marsh wildlife.

Deemed a number one wetland because of the diversity in its flora and fauna, Cooper Marsh is home to over 120 species of birds and waterfowl alone. Rare Black-crowned Night Herons can be found feeding in the marsh as can the Black Tern—also considered a diminishing species.

Serious bird-watchers willing to devote several days to the quest are sometimes lucky enough to find the Great Egret which feeds here during the summer months. This elusive bird is expanding its northern limits and is generally more at home in South America and the southern United States than in Canada.

Other species may also one day make their home at Cooper Marsh. Several fields adjacent to the marsh have been planted with wildflowers and sunflowers in hopes of attracting additional species, and two osprey nesting platforms have been erected.

Animals of the four-legged variety also reside in Cooper Marsh. Rabbit, squirrel, brush wolf, fox, mink, and lots of muskrat either make their home here or pass through regularly. Otter sightings indicate that they too may be finding a haven in this 650 acre wetland.

Although bird activity decreases in the winter months, other recreational opportunities present themselves. Trails remain open and cross-country skis and snow-shoes are a good way to see the marsh wildlife thriving here during our Canadian winters.

An interpretive center, which includes a display area that changes with each season and classrooms for large groups, is open every day. Trails are always available for early morning and evening walks when nature viewing is at its best. Individuals who wish to visit the marsh and walk the trails and 580 meters of boardwalks can do so at no cost. Fees are charged, however, for large groups and schools wishing guided tours or lectures.

G.E.

The Glendale Restaurant and Tavern, Summerstown

Our next destination is Summerstown, which you can reach by following Highway 2 west for 7.2 kilometers from Cooper Marsh.

Constructed some 80 years ago, the Glendale was originally a pool hall-turned-speakeasy where illicit alcohol was served in teacups. Now operated by Susan and Claude Bourck, it's renowned as the home of the best fried fish on the riverfront. Of special note are the mounted fish, including a huge 'Lancaster Perch' which grace its walls.

Fairfield House

Continue west from Summerstown along Highway 2 another 1.2 kilometers west to Fairfield House.

Fairfield is set back from the road on a rise of land overlooking the river. This beautifully ornate Italianate-style house was built in 1865 by John Angus Cameron, or *Cariboo* Cameron as he was known, at a cost of around $20,000. Constructed of painted brick the house has stone edging the corners.

**Gold prospector 'Cariboo' Cameron's Italianate style house, Fairfield House, built in 1865.
Photo by Pat MacKenna.**

Popular from 1850 to 1900, Italianate-style homes were distinguished by a belvedere, ornate cornice brackets, exuberant brick and stone work at the corners, and elaborate window cornices.

Since it was first built the house has undergone some radical external alterations. A modern brick wing now extends west from the back of the house. But when Fairfield was first built ornate wrought iron gates gave access to the circular drive in front of the house. The original veranda was constructed of wood and had French windows opening along its east and west walls. Bay windows decorated the east and west sides of the first floor and there were double casement windows in the front. The roof had a small octagonal tower with arched windows.

Inside, on the main floor, was a large dining room and drawing-room, with a long hall, and oval-shaped staircase. The kitchen was located at the rear. The second floor consisted of four main bedrooms. Additional servants' rooms were located at the back of the house with a rear staircase that connected them to the kitchen. On the third floor an unfinished attic with stairs led to the tower.

Cariboo Cameron's life was tragically ironic. He was a local farmer who, accompanied by his young wife Sophia and baby daughter, went out to the gold fields in British Columbia to seek his fortune in late 1861. The daughter died soon after their arrival and Sophia died a few months later. Before her death, Cameron promised his wife that he would take her body home for burial.

Two months after Sophia's death, Cariboo and his partners struck gold. Cameron stayed on for ten months to mine the gold. Now a very rich man, he returned home with the metal casket containing his wife's body preserved in alcohol.

Upon arrival in Cornwall he had the body buried without the casket being opened. Shortly after the funeral rumors began to circulate: Cameron's wife had not died but had been sold for a large sum of gold to a rich Indian chief. Finally, in desperation, Cameron had his wife's body exhumed to silence the gossip.

Built on land that had originally belonged to his family, Cameron named the house after his grandfather's old home. A few years after its completion, he married Christianne Woods.

Eighteen years later, due to bad business investments and over-generosity to family and friends, Cariboo found himself short of money, and in 1888 he and his wife returned to the gold fields in British Columbia only to find that there was no more gold. Cameron died of a stroke shortly after their arrival, and is buried in Camerontown, B.C.

Fairfield was privately owned until it was purchased by the Brothers of the Sacred Heart in 1945. They converted it into a boys' boarding school. The school is now closed and the building is not open to the public.

Outside a small church on the north side of the road .6 kilometers from Fairfield House there is another plaque commemorating the 260th anniversary of the Salem congregation, founded by the Reverend John Bethune, 1752-1815. Cariboo Cameron's beloved wife Sophia is buried in the graveyard there.

P.M.

Bed and Breakfast By the Sea

From Summerstown on, every bend in road brings another view of the river. A short distance west of Summerstown, about .3 kilometers from Salem Church, you will find Bed and Breakfast By The Sea. Accommodations are in a self-contained area of the house with a private bathroom and living room equipped with television and video. A full breakfast is served in the homey family kitchen or on the patio. You can do a bit of boat watching from either one. The owners John and Darlene Lounsbury are knowledgeable about the area's attractions, and there are boat docking facilities, swimming, and fishing on the premises.

Stone House Point

Continue west toward Cornwall along Highway 2 for another 3.8 kilometers to Stone House Point. A cairn and plaque have been erected there by the Historic Sites & Monuments Board of Canada to honor Colonel John MacDonell. He served with the Royal Highland Regiment and later Butler's Rangers. He represented Glengarry in the Legislative Assembly 1792-1800 and was chosen as the first Speaker of the Assembly. It was at Stone House Point, in 1791, that Colonel MacDonell built his residence, Glengarry House. The largest private residence in the Eastern District, the three storey home was destroyed by fire in 1813.

Behind the trees Stone House Point also offers a

Stone House Point ruins in 1959. Dating from 1791, this three storey residence was the largest in Eastern Ontario before being destroyed by a fire accidentally started by defending local militia in 1813. Photo courtesy S. D. & G. Historical Society, Inverarden Museum.

great prospect on the St. Lawrence River and Seaway. Cargo ships have passed this way for many years, but before the St. Lawrence Seaway was completed they were necessarily smaller due to the dimensions of the Cornwall Canal and locks. With those restrictions gone, and deeper channels dredged in the river, large ships from all over the world can be seen here on their way to or from the Great Lakes. The river has always been an integral part of life in this area with its mixture of year round homes and summer cottages.

I have golden memories of fishing expeditions in an ancient rowboat in the Stone House Point area. The trips were always preceded by the gathering of dew worms by flashlight the night before. We started out very early in the morning and traveled from Cornwall at a sedate pace because cars were a luxury in the 1930s and my father did not care to push his too hard. The boat had to be dragged out from under some bushes by the shore, and frogs were chased from under the seats. Arranging our gear was tricky because slow leaks in the bottom had to be considered. Father rowed and I bailed. But we felt lucky to have a rowboat while others fished from shore with long bamboo poles. I can't boast of any record catches because my fishing partner firmly believed that if the fish didn't bite within ten minutes, they weren't going to, so he constantly upped anchor and moved on, muttering that he had not come all the way from Ireland to let a bunch of perch toy with him! We puttered around the reed beds, ate our lunch, and sang old songs. A quick stop at Braunstein's market in Cornwall solved the problem of providing fish for supper, and no one in the family was ever crass enough to enquire why the catch of the day was so professionally filleted.

Today, as I watch fishermen in colorful metalic speedboats, sailboats chuffed with wind, water skiers leaving transient trails behind them, and happy houseboaters waving, I know the lure of the St. Lawrence is still strong and there are many golden memories in the making.

Other, less fortunate travelers, have taken away very different memories. As Elizabeth Simcoe wrote, on 24 June 1792:

> We arrived here about sunset, and at a small inn on the point (Pointe au Bodet on the north shore of Lake St. Francis) found the principal inhabitants of the Township of Glengarry (Highlanders in their national dress). They came to meet the Governor, who landed to speak to them. They preceded us in their boat, a piper with them, towards Glengarry House. Mr. McDonell's, where the gentlemen went, but the wooden awning of our boat being blown off by a violent and sudden squall arising, we were glad to make towards the shore as fast as possible at Pointe Mouille on Lake Francis, west of Pointe au Bodet, and thought ourselves lucky that the boat had not been overset. We met with a miserable, wretched, dirty room at a Highlander's, the only house within some miles.

On the 25th Mrs. Simcoe continued:

> We breakfasted with Mr. McDonell, four leagues from Pointe Mouille; his new house (Glengarry), he has not finished, and resides in that which he first erected on his ground. A Catholic priest, his cousin, was there, who has lived five years among the Iroquois Indians at St. Regis (near Cornwall). They have a church, and he performs divine service in the Iroquois, of which he is perfect master, and he says their attention to the church service is very great, and the women sing psalms remarkably well. After breakfast we proceeded a league to Coll. Gray's [now the site of Inverarden Museum], from whence the Governor went to the Isle of St. Regis, to visit with Indians at their village, where they received him with dancing in a fierce style, as if they wished to inspire the spectators with terror and respect for their ferocious appearance. We slept at Coll. Gray's, at Gray's Creek, four miles below Cornwall.
>
> E.C.

Inverarden Regency Cottage Museum

From Stone House Point, continue west 4.7 kilometers toward Cornwall. On the city's outskirts—3332 Montreal Road—you will find Inverarden Regency Cottage Museum.

The building sits surrounded by trees on land that overlooks the St. Lawrence River. The center box was the first part of the house to be constructed. Laid out with a center hall floor plan, the house follows Loyalist tradition by placing the domestic quarters in the basement.

Inverarden is described as a Regency Cottage and its characteristic features are the Georgian symmetry of the facade, accented by a neo-classical center door which is guarded by columns, flanked by sidelights, and highlighted by a wide elliptical fanlight. Other traditional features include: the stucco exterior; the four chimneys balanced on both sides of a shallow pitched hipped roof; the hidden second floor illuminated by rear and side dormers; the casement windows; and the dramatic setting.

History

Inverarden was built in 1816 for John McDonald who was known as *Le Bras Croche* because of his slightly crooked right arm.

McDonald was an old Nor'Wester, who had been with the company for 23 years when he retired. He was a comparatively rich man once he had sold his shares in the fur trade and finally decided to retire to the country as a landed gentleman.

McDonald purchased 750 acres of land at Gray's Creek on the St. Lawrence River five kilometers east of Cornwall. Here he constructed this rubble stone cottage. The east and west wings were added later. Originally the house measured 15 x 11 meters and

Inverarden Regency Cottage Museum, once the home of Nor'Westers John McDonald and John Duncan Campbell. Photo by Pat MacKenna.

contained an excavated basement with a kitchen, larder, and additional rooms for servants. The main floor included a dining room and drawing room separated by a hall and staircase; with two smaller rooms at the rear, probably bedrooms. The upper half-storey remained unfinished. The house was furnished with English and Canadian furniture; a dining table with matching chairs and sideboard, an *oeil-de-boeuf* mirror, two sofas, a secretaire-bookcase, a pair of pedestal style card tables, and a piano.

McDonald and his Métis wife, Nancy Small, moved into the house in the fall of 1816 and began having the land cleared. John called the house "Gart," after his ancestral home in Scotland.

As a wealthy man, McDonald was welcomed into Cornwall society, and was made a justice of the peace three years after his arrival. In 1818, he bought an additional 100 acre farm just east of his estate in Charlottenburgh Township.

In the spring of 1822, Eliza, his eldest daughter, married John Duncan Campbell a retired Nor'Wester, in Montreal. Campbell was forty-nine, only two years younger than McDonald; Eliza was eighteen. They came to live at Inverarden and started to raise a family. It was at this time that the east and west wings were added to the house, for the building was too small to house two families.

Shortly after his arrival in the area, John Duncan was appointed a magistrate in the Eastern District and became a Captain in the Stormont Militia.

Although he had been married to Nancy Small for twenty-four years, McDonald now decided to marry Amelia, a niece of Laird Hugh McGillis of Williamstown. (His previous marriage was an Indian ceremony.) Shortly after the wedding John sold Inverarden, along with 150 acres of land to Eliza for the sum of $5.00. With his new wife he moved into the farm that had been purchased in Charlottenburgh Township. This he also named Gart.

Eleven years later John Duncan died, leaving Eliza to care for three young children, look after her aging mother, and pay off a mortgage held on the farm by her brother-in-law Colin Campbell. Upon learning of his brother's death, Colin waived the debt.

Freed of this obligation, Eliza succeeded in managing the farm and providing for her family. She lived until the ripe old age of 86, dying in 1890. On her death the responsibility of operating the farm was assumed by her eldest son, James Reid.

Persuaded by a cousin Sir George Duncan Gibb that he was the rightful heir to the Earl of Breadalbane's estate, James traveled to England in 1871, to claim both the title and the land. His claim was not successful.

Upon his return from London James renamed the house "Inverardine." On the highest point of land where the family cemetery once existed, a view of Gray's Creek merging with the St. Lawrence River can be seen. Inverardine is the combination of two Gaelic words meaning the high headland where the river meets the sea. The name has gradually changed through the years to the present officially accepted title of Inverarden.

James devoted his life to farming. He married Mary Elizabeth Burke in 1875, when he was forty-nine and she was twenty-one. They had four sons: James Burke who died of pneumonia at the age of twelve, John Duncan, William Robertson, and James Ellis. The boys' mother died fifteen years after her marriage. James lived until 1912.

After their father's death the property was divided equally among the three sons. James Ellis sold his share to his brothers in 1919. John and William continued to share the house and farm the property until 1961.

The land was purchased by Chemcell Ltd. in 1965. Unfortunately, as it was unoccupied, the building was damaged by vandals. In 1968 the cottage was declared a national historic site, and was purchased by the Crown in 1972. Parks Canada undertook the restoration.

The house is now jointly leased to the City of Cornwall and the Stormont, Dundas, and Glengarry Historical Society. The refurnishing of the cottage has been undertaken by the Historical Society which refurnished the house circa 1830, and has operated it as a restored house museum and archives on behalf of the City of Cornwall since 1979. Admission is free.

P.M.

Story

Who was John McDonald of Garth?

Apprenticed as a clerk to the North West Company to earn his way in life John McDonald, as a young man, was warned by his granduncle to be "modest, mild and unaffecting to (his) Equals and even to Inferiors" as well as "affable and Courteous to all (he conversed) with." Immediately forgetting these instructions when he arrived in Canada in 1791, he issued two challenges to duels with pistols within his first six months here.

He never lost his truculence. To maintain order in the West, he always carried a pair of pocket pistols and a sword. He wrote in his autobiographic notes about the need for bravado to gain and keep the respect and cooperation of the French Canada voyageurs and the Natives.

In describing one hunting expedition he notes:

The bear had only two springs more to make to get to me, I had therefore a lucky escape . . . [The bear was shot by a companion] I could not run, in any case, as it would have ruined my character and destroyed my influence over the men forever. This influence had to be maintained by the utmost determination.

How much, however, can you believe? He admits in his autobiography, written 50 years after the events, that it must be "more egotistical than historical as a matter of course."

With a confession like this it is just possible we may never know the real John McDonald of Garth.

I.B.

John McDonald of Garth c. 1804 when McDonald would have been about 33 years old.
Photo courtesy Ontario Archives.

Lancaster Perch

And finally, no tour of this area would be truly complete without mention of the local fish delicacy, Lancaster Perch, which is plentiful in the waters of Lake St. Francis and the St. Lawrence River. These young perch, measuring ten or more inches, are carefully filleted in one piece to form a Y-shape. Five or more make a serving, while three fill a fish roll generously. In restaurants they are usually lightly dredged in seasoned flour and panfried. They are served with a cooked dressing. Area residents enjoy this delicacy at giant Perch Fries such as those hosted by the Royal Canadian Legion.

Wilfrid Montreuil has organized many a Lancaster Perch Fry in his time, for christenings and other summer get-togethers. His recipe calls for an open fire in an old washing machine shell over which is placed the grill and, finally, a huge cast iron fry pan. Melt a pound of butter and throw in lots of onions. When the onions become transparent, push them to the side and start frying your perch, shiny side of the fillet down to prevent curling. Season with plenty of salt and pepper.

As you can see, this is not for cholesterol counters! For the truly intrepid, fry some thick slices of French crusty bread; some aficionados insist on toasted hot dog rolls. The recipes for perch sauce abound in this neighborhood. Here is one of the best:

Perch Sauce

> *2 cups vinegar*
> *1 cup sugar*
> *butter the size of an egg*
> *1 teaspoon salt*
> *1 teaspoon Keen's mustard powder*
> *white pepper to taste*

> *Heat together. Meanwhile, beat 6 eggs lightly with 1 cup sour cream. Pour into the hot vinegar and let it all slowly thicken. This should be cooked in a double boiler. Keeps well, covered, in fridge.*

Lancaster Perch platters and rolls are served in local restaurants and chip wagons. Try some for lunch!

E.M.

Directions

A good feed of perch should fortify you for our next tour along the Fur Trade Route and into the mythology of Canada's most famous explorers, surveyors, and entrepreneurs—the Nor'Westers.

CHAPTER 2

The Fur Trade Route

Preamble

Discovering and laying claim to half of a continent, the Montreal fur traders first directed by the French and then appropriated by the Scots under the banner of the North West Company, dominated early British North America's social and economic life. Every spring the fur brigades started out from Lachine north along the Ottawa River to the Mattawa and then west to the annual rendezvous at Fort William to exchange furs and trade goods, to count profits and plan new stratagems for the coming year. Earning vast fortunes, many of the partners, the sons of Loyalists, upon retirement returned home to Greater Glengarry to assume the life of landed gentlemen.

Author Pat MacKenna traces the route of the fur trade from Lachine, Quebec to Pointe Fortune on the Ottawa River, and then south into Loyalist

Glengarry County, to the homes and museums dedicated to Simon Fraser, David Thompson, John McDonell, and their partners, neighbors, and kinsmen. No mere armchair traveler herself, Pat came to North America in 1965 on an extended holiday from Britain to see "how the other half of the world lived." Pat stayed and followed in the footsteps of her great Aunt Bird, who penned Victorian travel books and rode across Morocco on a horse at age 70. A professional photographer and writer, Pat will now take you to the "heart" of Greater Glengarry County!

I.B.

History: The Fur Traders of Eastern Ontario

Simon Fraser, David Thompson, Alexander MacKenzie, John McDonell "le pretre" (the priest), William McGillivray, Finan McDonald, and their partners in the North West Company are — or should be — Canadian household names. As venturers, explorers, and mapmakers, they traversed and mapped present day Western Canada in search of the fabled Northwest Passage and beaver pelts. Just the mere mention of their names conjures up images of brave adventurers traveling across North America in canoes, on foot, over plains and mountains, discovering and laying claim to half of the continent for the British Crown. In truth, though, while these men carried out these exploits and more, they were simply satisfying the dictates of European fashion and

THE FUR TRADE ROUTE

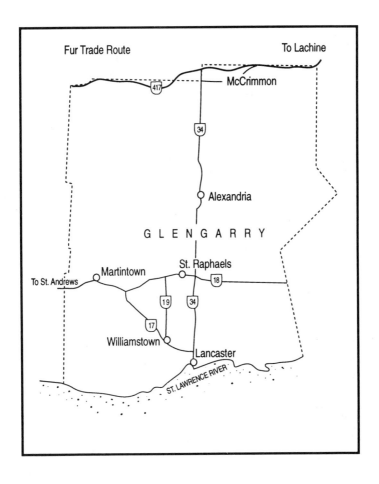

searching for beavers for the minutely barbed hairs of their pelts which would be turned into felt for men's hats.

Spreading out along the old French trade routes from Montreal and beyond Fort William, the Nor' Westers came into inevitable conflict with the Hudson's Bay men, and at times appeared to act more like buccaneers than merchants. In 1821 when the two firms amalgamated the rivalry ended.

While some of these men left the service before the merger, many suddenly retired as a result of it, and after years of daring exploits and sometimes violent encounters, they disappeared from the pages of history. Where did they go? Many of the most prominent Nor' Westers went home to Eastern Ontario to live as Lairds.

The fur trade in Canada was initiated by the Hudson's Bay Company, an English trading corporation formed in 1670. It was granted the "Monopoly of trade through the Hudson Strait" by Charles II. The boundaries of the Company's territory were never clearly defined, but were understood to extend from Labrador to the Rocky Mountains, and from the headwaters of the Red River to Chesterfield Inlet on the Hudson Bay. In the late 17th century the Company established a number of posts on the shores of James and Hudson Bays.

The North West Company, founded in Montreal in 1783-84, soon became the Hudson's Bay Company's chief competitor. The Nor' Westers originally confined their operations to the Lake Superior region and the valleys of the Red, Assiniboine, and Saskatchewan Rivers, but later spread north and west to the shores of the Arctic and Pacific oceans. Their wilderness headquarters was located at Grand Portage on Lake Superior. This was transferred to Fort Kamanistiquia in 1803, later renamed Fort William.

Intense rivalry existed between the two organizations, and competition became bitter when the English company effectively cut off the North West Company's lines of communication by establishing a colony on the Red River in 1811-12. Open warfare broke out shortly afterwards when Nor'Westers and Métis massacred the Red River colonists at Seven Oaks. In retaliation the Hudson's Bay men captured Fort William and destroyed Fort Gibraltar. Finally the two firms were forced to merge in 1821 by the British Government as the Hudson's Bay Company.

The assistance that the explorers obtained from the North American native peoples is frequently overlooked when discussing the fur trade and the subsequent exploration of Canada. The traders' practice of taking "Indian" wives helped greatly to cement relations between the two parties, but it was the adoption of the Natives' practical skills that was of greatest benefit to the traders. The Natives introduced traders to the birch-bark canoe, the snowshoe, toboggan, and the dog team. Natives taught them about wild rice and corn, and how to fish through the ice in winter. With the discovery of the method of preserving meat (pemmican), more time could be spent traveling and less hunting. Information on canoe routes came from the Natives. Without this knowledge, most of the exploration that occurred in the 18th and 19th centuries would never have been possible.

Native and European traders had different perspective on which party benefited most from this exchange, as the two following comments suggest:

> The people of the Countrie came flocking aboard, and brought us... Bevers skinnes, and Otter skinnes, which we bought for Beads, Knives ... Hatchets, (and other) trifles.
> — Robert Juet, 1609

> The English have no sense; they give us twenty knives like this for one Beaver skin.
> — a Montagnais Native, 1634

In her book *The North West Company*, historian Marjorie Wilkins Campbell summed up the Company by saying:

> The North West Company never was a company in the modern sense. It had no charter. It was, rather a series of co-partnerships between small groups of men who were promoters, merchants or fur-trader-explorers, or all three together or in turn. Some were French Canadian, others came from Montreal during the unsettled years of the American War of Independence. Most were Highland Scots.
>
> In the sense that most great events stem from comparatively small and obscure causes, a fashion in men's hats led to the formation of the North West Company—and the eventual discovery of the vast northwest.

THE FUR TRADE ROUTE

All trade goods going from or coming to North West Company headquarters in Montreal had to pass through the Lachine Canal. Our journey along the Fur Traders' Route naturally begins at Lachine, in the historic Fur Traders' Warehouse situated on the banks of the old canal.

Directions

This tour begins in Lachine. From Cornwall take Highway 401 east to Highway 20 which leads to Dorion. From Montreal take Highway 20 to 32nd Avenue in Lachine. Then turn left on Victoria Street, right on to 15th Avenue, and left again at St. Joseph Boulevard. A few hundred meters farther on is the site of the Fur Traders' Warehouse.

The Fur Traders' Warehouse

This historic building lies snug and compact on the banks of the old Lachine Canal. Located on a small island, it is separated from the road by a narrow channel. It was built in 1803 on behalf of the North West Company for the storage of fur and trade goods. When the North West company merged with the Hudson's Bay Company, the building became Bay headquarters between 1833-1859. Parks Canada purchased the warehouse in 1977 from the Sisters of Ste. Anne, who were using it as a residence for their employees. Today it is a museum that commemorates the fur trade.

**The Fur Traders' Warehouse on the south bank of the Lachine Canal was built in 1803.
Photo by Pat MacKenna.**

THE FUR TRADE ROUTE

Confronting you as you enter the warehouse are burlap packages, wooden barrels, boxes, and small kegs grouped in piles upon the floor. Fur pelts and iron traps hang from one wall. A map portraying the fur trading routes and the trading posts established by both companies dominates another wall. Looking at this map one can't help but marvel at the courage and tenacity that drove men like Alexander MacKenzie, Simon Fraser, and David Thompson who dreamed of finding a river passage to the Pacific Ocean, and in pursuit of that dream explored and mapped this country.

Portraits of the senior partners responsible for operating the company, *the bourgeois*, hang in the museum. Among the more famous are Simon McTavish, Sir Alexander MacKenzie, and William MacGillivray. The coat of arms of the North West Company is on display, a shield within whose upper half five voyageurs paddle a canoe and, in the lower half, a merchant ship sails across the ocean.

On a platform a mannequin in voyageur's clothing stoops under the weight of the pack he is carrying. One man could portage two packs at a time, each weighing approximately 40.5 kilos, or if he wanted to show off, three.

The *canot de maitre*, or master canoes, used on the Great Lakes and the Ottawa River, were about 11 meters long, 1.8 meters wide, and capable of carrying a gross weight of 3.63 tonnes. The *canot du nord*, or northern canoes, used on the smaller rivers between Lakes Superior and Athabasca, had half this capacity. The master canoes had approximately nine crew members and the northern canoes between five and six. These boats, constructed of birch-bark, had a life expectancy of a year.

Distance was a major problem for the North West Company. The English shipped their pelts to Europe from Hudson Bay, the Nor'Westers shipped theirs from Montreal. The Athabasca country, where the best quality pelts came from, was 4800 kilometers from Montreal. A freight canoe only averaged about 1600 kilometers per month and there were five months between break-up and freeze-up. To overcome the problems of time and distance, the Nor'Westers built their *entrepot* at Grand Portage on Lake Superior. This was later transferred to Fort William, when the American-Canadian border was established. The post was the annual rendezvous point between the Northerners, who had wintered in the west and came to the depot laden with furs, and the men from Lachine, who brought food and trade goods. For one month in the summer the depot became the largest 'city' in Upper Canada while the men traded, relaxed, celebrated, and made plans for the following year.

In the museum is a replica of a Beaver Club gold medal that belonged to James McGill. It commemorates his first visit to the north west in 1766. The Beaver Club was an exclusive club founded in 1785 by the fur traders of Montreal. Membership was conferred only when proof of having *wintered* in the west was obtained.

The Club dinners, held in the city, commenced on the first Wednesday in December and continued every fortnight until early April or May. Attendance was mandatory, the rules stating that "No member shall have a party at his home on the day the Club meets, nor accept invitations elsewhere but if in town must attend unless prevented by illness." The gold medallions had to be worn by all members on club nights. Engraved on the medal was the picture of a canoe shooting the rapids. Encircling the picture was the inscription, "Fortitude in distress."

During the evening a sumptuous meal would be served, and large quantities of wine, ale, and spirits would be consumed. Part of tradition was to try to drink each other under the table. There were five obligatory toasts "To the Mother of all Saints," "The King," "The Fur Trade and all its Branches," "Wives and Children," "Absent Members." After dinner the "calumet," the Native peace pipe, was passed around the table. A chosen member would then relate tales of adventures in Native country. Voyageur songs were sung in French ending with an ear splitting war-whoop. Often a "Grand Voyage" would be performed; members seated themselves in rows on the floor pretending that they were paddling canoes up a northern river. Swords, walking-sticks, or anything that came to hand were used to simulate paddles. The dinners ended when the large freight canoes left Lachine on their long journey to Grand Portage.

Returning to the outside of the warehouse, you can see that the narrow channel that separates the warehouse from the road is a canal. This is part of the original canal that was built between 1821-1825 to by-pass the Lachine Rapids. The wider channel, to the south of the warehouse, was constructed in 1841-1862. To prevent navigation coming to a standstill during construction, the new canal was built alongside the old.

If when you leave the warehouse, you turn east and walk half a kilometer, you will see on the south side of the road, a newly renovated, solitary two storey stone building, which was the first Inn to be constructed in Lachine. It was built by Hugh Henney in 1765, and soon became the voyageurs' favorite watering hole.

Continue walking east until you come to a small park on the banks of the canal owned by Parks Canada. From here the older canal can be seen branching from the wider one. Within the park there is a building called the Monk Pavilion which houses an exhibition showing the principal stages of the canal's history.

Return now to the warehouse parking lot. From here we shall travel to Bout de l'Isle, or Ste-Anne-de-Bellevue as it is called today. Simon Fraser owned a house there; and a small church once existed in Bout de l'Isle where voyageurs landed to say a final prayer and receive a blessing before setting off on their long hazardous journey. Our journey to this town takes us along the "Route Panoramique."

Route Panoramique

To reach Ste-Anne-de-Bellevue, turn west along St. Joseph Boulevard. As you leave the parking lot, keep the canal on your left and follow signs that direct you along the lake. This is the 30 kilometer long

Simon Fraser's House was originally built between 1798 and 1804. Photo by Pat MacKenna.

"Route Panoramique." As you travel through Lachine you will find a string of small parks that follows the water's edge, giving unrestricted views of the river.

About 1.5 kilometers west of the warehouse is Parc St-Louise, with an old quay and lighthouse. If you stop and walk out along the quay, you will see to the west the large expanse of Lac-Ste-Louise widening out before you, and to the east, far in the distance, you will see the Mercier Bridge crossing the St. Lawrence River above the Lachine Rapids.

Follow Lakeshore until you reach Parc Pointe-Claire Venture on the "Baie de Valois." From here, there is direct access to Highway 20. Take Highway 20 west and exit at Ste-Anne-de-Bellevue. Descend the exit ramp and turn left under the highway. Follow St. Pierre Boulevard to the intersection with Ste-Anne. Turn right and travel west through the village until you reach the overpass crossing the river. On the left is a parking lot with a view of the canal and the open river beyond. On the right, at 153 Ste-Anne-Boulevard, lies the Simon Fraser house, our next stop on the tour.

Simon Fraser House

The date of construction of the Simon Fraser House is debatable — some historians place it at 1798, others at 1804. The house was originally surrounded by a small two acre park with a garden and orchard. It now stands within a white picket fence, with three Lombardy poplars rising tall above the roof of the house, and two cedars guarding the path to the front door. Six dormer windows project snugly from the cedar shake roof with four rectangular windows on the ground floor. A porch protects the white front door which has six window lights in its upper half. The house is operated as a restaurant by the Auxiliary of the Victorian Order of Nurses (V.O.N.) and called the "Petit Café."

When you enter the building you will find yourself in a large L-shaped room with a fireplace at either end. The broad-axe marks are clearly visible on the hand-hewn beams that support the ceiling, and the thickness of the stone walls can be judged by the deep window recesses. The polished pine floor gives off a mellow glow.

The Simon Fraser who owned this house was not the famous explorer who discovered the Fraser River in British Columbia, but another Fraser. His father was Captain Alexander Fraser of Boleskine in Inverness, and his mother was Janet MacGillivray, daughter of Alexander MacGillivray of Aberchallader. Born in Scotland in about 1760, Simon came to Canada as a youth. In 1789 he operated a fur trading post in the English River area. Although not employed by the North West Company, he leased a post from them. He became a partner in the Company when he purchased a 1/46th share in 1795. He retired from active service in 1799, and resigned his share in the Company in 1805. In 1803 he joined the Beaver Club and remained a member until 1816. In 1804 Simon married Catherine McKay, whose two brothers William and Alexander were partners in the North West Company. He purchased the fief Bellevue on Lac des Deux Montagnes in 1807; and lived there until it burned down in 1820. He purchased this house in Ste-Anne-de Bellevue from Peter Grant, another partner in the North West Company. He continued to live there until his death in 1839. The house remained in the family's possession until it was acquired by Canadian Heritage of Quebec in 1961-62.

Leaving the Simon Fraser House, walk over and take a look at the canal and the lock, located a few hundred meters to the northwest of the house. Here the Ottawa River spills into the Lac des Deux Montagnes and is then channeled through the narrow passage separating Ile Perrot and the "Bout de l'Isle" into Lac St Louis, creating the Ste-Anne Rapids.

The Ste-Anne Lock now enables boats to sail between Lac St Louis and the Lac des Deux Montagnes by avoiding the rapids. The first canal was not built until 1816, so it was of use only in the latter days of the fur trade.

If you stand at the north end of Ste-Anne Lock and look over the broadening expanse of water to where the bridge that carries Highway 40 spans Lac des Deux Montagnes, the outline of the Laurentian Mountains can be seen on the horizon.

Returning to the road you will see the gray stone church of Ste-Anne-De-Bellevue. To the north of this, on the shore of the lake, a convent once stood. This has since been pulled down and replaced by modern senior citizens' residence. In 1969, E.W. Morse in his book on Canadian fur trade routes commented upon this convent:

The stone convent at Ste-Anne, built at the head of the present canal, was recently examined by an architect, who found considerable evidence to support local rumour that its bottom storey was in fact the little church where the voyageurs landed and left their "mite" to receive the priest's blessing for their hazardous journey to the "pays d'en haut."

Unfortunately, nothing remains of the old convent.

Our next destination is Pointe Fortune on the Ottawa River, the site of Captain John McDonell's House.

Captain John McDonell's House

Continue west along Ste-Anne Boulevard past the residential area. Follow the road as it veers right and becomes a one-way thoroughfare. At the lights, turn left onto St. Pierre Boulevard and then turn onto Route 40. Take Route 40 West and cross Lac des Deux Montagnes bridge. When the road divides, follow Route 40 for approximately 38 kilometers. Take Exit #2 for Pointe Fortune. Follow the signs through the village, keeping the Ottawa River on the right. The road climbs, and half way up the hill, on your right standing above the river, you will find a large two storey stone building. The windows are boarded up and it is surrounded by a rusty fence topped with barbed wire. A "No Trespassing" sign is nailed to one wall. The property is owned by the Ontario Heritage

Pointe Fortune, John McDonell's home and trading post, was constructed in 1817. Photo by Pat MacKenna.

Foundation, and the security precautions are to prevent further vandalism.

It is difficult to visualize this as having been the luxurious Georgian mansion built in 1817 for Captain John McDonell, or "le pretre" as he was often known. Elder son of John McDonell of Scothouse—"Spanish John"—and brother to Miles McDonell the first Governor of Assiniboia.

McDonell had been a partner in the North West Company for sixteen years when he retired in 1812. He came to this location a few years later, with Magdeleine Poitras his Métis wife. It was here that he started a commercial enterprise that finally extended half a mile along the banks of the Ottawa River. McDonell opened a general store, built a grist mill, a frame saw-mill, an ice-house, smoke house, and sheds. Acting as a freight forwarder for goods between Hull and Montreal, he also sponsored the first steamboat on the Ottawa River. In 1816 he served in the Upper Canada House of Assembly. McDonell died in April 1850, and lies buried in the Roman Catholic cemetery at St. Andrews, Quebec. He and his wife had a total of six sons and two daughters.

From here we move onto the village of Williamstown, in Glengarry County, a distance of some 73 kilometers.

Williamstown

Continue past the house at Pointe Fortune, turn left and continue three kilometers to Route 40 west to

Ottawa. Route 40 becomes Ontario's Highway 417. Take exit 27, follow Route 34 south to Alexandria and Green Valley. At the flashing yellow light at Brown House Corner, turn west onto County Road 18. Travel five kilometers to County Road 19, turn south, and follow the road to Williamstown.

As you will discover, quite a few Nor'Westers were either born in, or retired to, Glengarry County and the Williamstown area. Williamstown was named after Sir William Johnson the celebrated Indian Superintendent. His son Sir John Johnson escaped from the Mohawk Valley in New York in 1776 accompanied by many of his loyal supporters. Upon arrival in Montreal he formed the King's Royal Regiment of New York and fought for the Loyalist cause in the American War of Independence. In recognition of his services and to compensate for his massive land losses in New York State, Johnson was given extensive Crown land grants in Glengarry County.

The Caron House, a highly regarded bed and breakfast, is an appropriate place to begin a tour of the village. You may choose to rest the night here before taking in the other sites at this stop on the Fur Traders Route.

To find the Caron House, pass through the main intersection in the village, and continue south across the Raisin River. At a 'Y' fork in the road, keep right. Then bear left on County Road 19 and the Caron House is on the east side of the road, opposite St. Mary's Church.

Hugh McGillis, an ex-Nor'Wester, had this house

built in 1837 for his unmarried sister Mary. It is a charming two storey brick house that stands in its own small garden close to the road. The front of the house has a peak-roofed vestibule with an attractive oval shaped gable window above it. At the back is a large sunny veranda with wicker chairs.

As you will discover when you enter the house, the old world atmosphere is enhanced by an attractive collection of antique furniture. There are several unusual features about the place. For example there is no main hall, and the stairs are located to the rear of the house in what was once the kitchen, now called the den. Both the dining and living room have tin ceilings while the old kitchen has a cross and bible door leading to the veranda outside. The wainscoting is unusually deep, and all the interior door locks—with one exception—are upside down, whether by design or accident is unknown. The windows have interior shutters.

You may notice that there is no outside handle to the front door. This was considered unnecessary for people of affluence as servants were always on hand to open the door to either the owner or visitors.

Upstairs there are two rooms available for guests, with double brass bedsteads in each, and sloped ceilings that enhance the country atmosphere. The bathroom contains an old style pedestal bath and a wash-basin with brass and ceramic fittings.

St. Mary's Catholic Church is located directly across the road from Caron House. Unpretentious in style, it was built from local stone between 1847-49. The

The central portion of the Johnson-McGillis House was built around 1784, making it one of the oldest houses in Ontario. Photo by Pat MacKenna.

eastern end is semicircular and the windows are Gothic in style. At the north entrance the three large wooden doors are painted blue and white. The steeple is hexagonal with an ornate metal cross at its tip.

Four acres of land were donated by Nor'Wester Hugh McGillis for the construction of the church, presbytery, and cemetery. His body lies within the church, and a tablet above the choir-stalls marks his grave. A striking feature of the church interior is the hand-painted ceiling by the Panzerommi Brothers of New York. They renovated and redecorated the interior in 1916. The Indian sacrifice of Fathers Brebeuf and Lalemont is portrayed in the stained glass window on the west side of the sanctuary.

Originally built as a mission to relieve the parish of St. Raphaels, St. Mary's did not establish independence until 1854.

The Manor House, built originally by Sir John Johnson and later purchased by Hugh McGillis, is another important historical site in the village. To reach The Manor House return towards the bridge but do not cross it. Continue down the street past the fire station and the Township Office until the road ends. On the right you will see a cedar-lined drive and a large white house. This is the Manor House.

Hugh McGillis was born in Scotland in 1769 and in 1773 emigrated with his parents to New York. They moved to Glengarry as United Empire Loyalists after the American War of Independence. McGillis joined the North West Company in 1790 and became a partner eleven years later. After serving in many different posts he retired from the Company in 1816 and returned to Glengarry with his Métis wife.

In 1818 he bought the Manor House at Williamstown—thought to have been built in 1784—and the adjoining farmland from Sir John Johnson. Hugh became known locally as *Laird McGillis* because he owned so much property in the village. It is believed that McGillis' wife and family returned to the west when he settled in Williamstown. The east wing was built by his nephew who inherited the house in 1849.

Today the white painted Manor House stands on a grassy knoll high above the river, protected to the south and west by tall cedars. To the east, below a high bank, the Raisin River rushes through a narrowing channel. Once a grist and saw mill built by Johnson stood on the opposite bank.

Designated a historic site in 1969, the house is now maintained by Parks Canada. At present only the east wing is open to the public as a county library.

St. Andrew's United Church is also closely connected to the history of the fur trade. To reach this church, retrace your route past the Township Office, turn right, and cross the bridge. At the stop sign turn right, travel east on John Street, and turn left on to Church Street.

St. Andrew's was founded by the "father" of Presbyterianism in Upper Canada, John Bethune. The Church became a "United" church in 1925 when several denominations joined forces.

Bethune was born in 1751 on the island of Skye

and educated at King's College in Aberdeen. He emigrated to North Carolina about 1773, where he was imprisoned by the Rebels during the War of Independence. Upon release he traveled to Halifax, and then Montreal where he established a Presbyterian church. He arrived in Glengarry in 1787, where he established yet another church.

His wife, Veronica Wadden, was the elder daughter of Jean Etienne Wadden, a North West Company partner who was killed by Nor'Wester Peter Pond in 1782 at Lac la Ronge.

The first Presbyterian church built at Williamstown was constructed of logs. It was replaced in 1804 by a stone church that collapsed due to poor construction in 1809. The present church was built from fieldstone between 1812 and 1818. Unfortunately Bethune died before its completion.

The church bell was donated by Sir Alexander MacKenzie in 1806. Although he never lived here, MacKenzie owned over 800 acres of land in the county, and had an uncle who settled here in 1784. When the church was completed, six pews were set aside for MacKenzie and five of the retired Nor' Westers who lived in the area. John MacGillivray and Duncan Cameron, two old North West partners, are buried in the graveyard, as are many United Empire Loyalists. To commemorate the latter, St. Andrew's Church was designated a "Loyalist" church in June 1980, and was presented with a "Loyalist" flag. The flag stands within the church near the dais.

St. Andrew's United Church was built between 1812 and 1818 and is constructed of fieldstone. Photo by Pat MacKenna.

> Tread softly, stranger, reverently, draw near the vanguard of a nation slumbers here.

These simple but very evocative lines speak volumes. They portray in a subtle yet simple manner the degree of respect that is due to the pioneers who lie buried in this graveyard.

To commemorate the arrival of the United Empire Loyalists, a delicate bronze statue on a stone plinth can be seen to the north of the paved walk leading to the church. Called simply *Arrival, United Empire Loyalist 1782*, it shows a man kneeling on the ground praying, while a saddled horse grazes contentedly beside him.

The church and the graveyard slumber peacefully, surrounded by a wrought iron railing. Dominating the paved walk leading to the main entrance are two large elms. The stone walls of the church have a mellow hue and the doors and windows are painted an avocado green with white trim. The metal roof supports an octagonal bell-tower crowned with a copper weathercock. The round-headed Palladian style windows with two small rose windows located high in the east and west gables are among some of the most attractive features of this church.

On a lighter note, a carved wooden owl perched high to the left of the main door can be seen leaning forward slightly; it appears to be watching people as they enter.

The wooden gallery is one of the first things that impresses as you enter the church. Supported by eight wooden pillars, it runs the length of the north, south, and west walls. An impression of delicacy is created by the carving that decorates its surface. The pews are made of highly polished ash; those against the walls are aligned towards the dais. Before the church was modernized in 1882, there were rows of box pews that opened out into tables with seats on either side for Communion.

Against the northeast wall are three glass cabinets. One contains the Communion plate, another the Bicentennial Communion tokens from Fayetteville Presbytery North Carolina—once Bethune's parish—the third houses a square silver box, with the Reverend John Bethune's name engraved upon its lid.

Now climb to the gallery. Here are additional pews and an unimpeded view of the 19th-century wrought iron chandelier. In addition there are eight double-bracketed oil lamps that stand on long slim stems around the gallery. Nine electric lamps suspended from the ceiling have superseded their use. The lofty barrel-vaulted ceiling, an unusual feature, is made of polished bass-wood.

Descending now to the main floor, walk through to the vestry at the east end of the church. Here you can see portraits of Bethune and various other ministers who have served the church. There is also a framed copy of the original petition sent to the General Assembly of the Church of Scotland in 1821 requesting permission to form a Presbytery. Now let's move on to the house where Bethune once lived.

Bethune-Thompson House is located on John Street. Return to John Street and continue east, around a sharp left bend. A sign on the right alerts you to the Bethune-Thompson House.

The house was first owned by John Bethune and then by David Thompson, the famous cartographer, explorer, and partner in the North West Company. It features a mixture of architectural styles, the oldest section being the original kitchen, thought to date from the 1780s. The central portion of the house was built in 1805 as the manse for John Bethune. When he bought the house from Bethune's widow in 1815, Thompson added the front veranda, renovated the front dormer, and altered the eave and roof lines. The house is basically Georgian with some French and German influence. Between 1912-25 the north wing was demolished and replaced by the two storey gambrel roof section with a verandah to the west.

The house was purchased by the Ontario Heritage Foundation in 1977, and has since been renovated. It is open to the public on Sundays.

The interior contains a box hall, a rarity in Ontario, and the staircase has a goose-neck hand rail. Some of the oldest remaining examples of wallpaper in the Province of Ontario can be seen in this house, dating back to Bethune's time. The parlor has a beautiful Georgian mantelpiece. In the dining room, if you look very carefully, you can discern the letter T scratched into one of the panes of glass. Possibly one of the thirteen Thompson children, bored by being confined indoors, whiled away some time carving his initial into the glass. Off the dining room is Thompson's office where he drew many of his maps. The walls are still painted the original shade of green.

A 1912 photograph of Bethune-Thompson House, known from the middle of the 19th century until fairly recently as the 'White House.' The right-hand wing of the original Loyalist structure dates from circa 1784. Photo courtesy of the Public Archives of Canada (51909).

Thompson settled here with his Métis wife, Charlotte Small, and their children. During his nineteen year stay, Thompson farmed the property. He was also employed by the International Boundary Commission for ten years surveying the border between Canada and the United States. A local store that he and his sons operated in Williamstown proved a financial disaster. In 1835 the house had to be sold, and Thompson moved to Longueuil, Quebec, where he died in 1857 at the age of 87. His body lies buried in the Mount Royal Protestant Cemetery in Montreal. A simple monument, consisting of a sextant upon a fluted column, was erected over his grave by the Canadian Historical Association in 1927.

Nor'Westers and Loyalist Museum is located on John Street, west from the Bethune-Thompson House, past the main intersection, on the north side of the street.

The museum is an attractive Georgian style structure constructed of brick on land donated by Sir John Johnson. It was built as a combined public school and high school in 1862, and continued operating as a school until 1965.

The museum was founded in 1967 as a Canadian Centennial Project to honor both the fur trade and the United Empire Loyalists. It contains artifacts that relate to the early pioneers of the area and to the fur trade. To assist you, the museum provides a small booklet containing a condensed version of the exploits of the Nor'Westers who retired to the Williamstown area.

The Nor'Westers and Loyalist Museum was built in 1862 to house a school that closed in 1965. Photo by Pat MacKenna.

THE FUR TRADE ROUTE

The ground floor is devoted to United Empire Loyalist memorabilia and artifacts. Among these is a map showing the route the Loyalists took when they escaped from the Mohawk Valley in New York and fled to St. Regis with Sir John Johnson. Also on view is a plan showing the lot numbers that were assigned to the original Loyalist settlers in the first land survey made by Patrick McNiff in 1786. A montage of drawings portraying life in pioneer days leaves little doubt that pioneer life was hard. The many artifacts on display depict the type of clothing worn, as well as the equipment and utensils available at the time.

Upstairs there are artifacts from the fur trade. Among these are David Thompson's writing desk and a copy of his map of the Northwest, showing the transportation routes between Lake Ontario and the Pacific Ocean. This map was compiled by Thompson based on his own surveys, and those of Philip Turnor, Sir Alexander MacKenzie, and John Stuart, between 1792-1812. The original map hung at Fort William for many years. Also on view is a replica of an 8 meter North West, birch-bark canoe, made by the Natives of Manonan, Quebec and used on a trip between Grand Portage and Williamstown in 1967.

There are examples of items that would have been traded with the Natives. A Hudson's Bay Table of Barter shows that four beaver pelts were worth one gallon of brandy and eleven purchased a gun.

One small item worth noting is a framed copy of the *Subscription of the Gentlemen of the North West Co. for the building of the Church of St. Andrew's.*

The subscription raised funds for the stone church constructed at St. Andrews West. Among the signatures listed are those of John McDonell who retired to Pointe Fortune, Hugh McGillis, John McGillivray of Williamstown, and Simon Fraser who retired to St. Andrews West.

Dalcrombie, a house once owned by John McGillivray, is our next stop. Continue west on John Street—now County Road 17—to the intersection with County Road 27. Turn south, cross MacGillivray bridge, and Dalcrombie is on the left.

McGillivray named his house Dalcrombie after his birthplace in Scotland. It has been renamed "Avondbloem" by its present owners. This is a private home that is not open to the public, but it is visible from the road. The cream-colored house stands back from the highway among pine and spruce trees. A short gravel drive curves in front of the main entrance to the house.

John McGillivray purchased the property in 1818, after his retirement from the North West Company, for the sum of £1450 from Thomas Munro, a Loyalist. The property then consisted of 241 acres with a simple frame house built around 1800.

In 1819, the same year that he was appointed Commissioner for Crown Lands, John married Isabella McLean, daughter of the Hon. Neil McLean of St. Andrews West. He was in his forties and she was twenty. They had a total of four daughters, all of whom died shortly after birth, and four sons who survived.

There were a further two sons:

> One winter in a wild storm, there was a knock at the door, Isabella opened it and there stood an Indian woman with two small boys. She had come from the far north-west, all the way to Glengarry to claim their rights for the two boys. Mrs. McGillivray rose to the occasion like a Christian and a lady, and took the wanderers in. When spring came, the woman left for the west. John and Isabella kept the two boys. One is thought to have died in childhood.

Whether these boys were born of the same mother as William and Elizabeth is not known. Mrs. van Beek goes on to say that Ian Henderson, a local resident, recalls having been told by his aunt that she had seen the Native son of John McGillivray working as a clerk in nearby Vankleek Hill.

McGillivray constructed a new house in 1821 that incorporated the Munro house as a kitchen and storage area. He was much involved with local affairs; he was a ruling elder at St. Andrew's Presbyterian church in Williamstown, and subscribed to the building of the Presbyterian Church at Martintown. He was Justice of the Peace for Charlottenburgh, and Commissioner for Affidavits. From 1839-1841 he was a member of the Upper Canada Legislative Council.

In 1855, three years before his death, he traveled to Scotland to claim the estate and chieftainship of the McGillivray clan. He did not live to see this claim realized. His elder son Neil John inherited the title in 1857. In 1905 Carrie Macgillivray (the family had changed the spelling of the name by this time for reasons unknown), a granddaughter, had extensive renovations made to the house. The Munro house was demolished; the foundations were raised, and a large gable was built at the front, with a wide veranda below. Two chimneys were removed from the east and west walls and replaced by one central chimney. Inside, certain doors were replaced by arches to ensure better heat circulation.

Before leaving the Williamstown area, you may wish to fortify yourself with food, drink, and good cheer at Jack Delaney's Pub and Restaurant, located on John Street near the bridge. Here amateur musicians might be playing traditional tunes on the piano, or local crooners may be singing ancient ballads. The patio view over the Raisin River is relaxing. Naturally, Lancaster Perch is available on the menu.

St. Andrews West

Now we travel on to St. Andrews West, a distance of 16.6 kilometers. It was here that Simon Fraser, a partner in the North West Company and the famous explorer of the Fraser River in British Columbia chose to retire.

Take County Road 27 north to the intersection at McQuaig's Corners, turn west on the County Road 18, and follow this road to Martintown and then St. Andrews West. The historic village center is located at the intersection with Highway 138.

John Sandfield Macdonald Quinn's Inn was erected in 1865 as a hotel for politician John Sandfield Macdonald. A country store when this photograph was taken around 1900, proprietors Elizabeth and William Masterston are shown on the front steps.
Photo Courtesy of the Ontario Archives (AO-130).

There is a story that the Loyalist settlers arrived here on St. Andrew's Day. Alternatively as the village was settled by Highland Scots, and St. Andrew is the patron saint of Scotland, what better name could be chosen?

When you reach the village you may be ready for some refreshment. Continuing in the pioneer tradition, why don't you try the John Sandfield Macdonald Quinn's Inn? The Inn serves soup and sandwiches and one main dish. Renovations to the Inn were completed in April 1991 and the building has been designated of historic and architectural value. The exterior of the building now appears as it did in 1900.

This inn was built in 1865 as a hotel and tavern for John Sandfield Macdonald, Prime Minister of the Province of Canada, and the first Premier of Ontario. The hotel was strategically placed on what was then the main stagecoach and military highway between Montreal, Kingston, and Toronto. Macdonald never operated the hotel himself; it was leased to others on condition that the basement be kept as a banqueting hall to be used by the villagers. Between 1895-1989 the building operated as a store. After 96 years, the building is now returning to its original purpose.

The village of St. Andrews contains one of the oldest remaining stone structures—originally built as a Roman Catholic church—in the province of Ontario, now used as the parish hall. This is the church towards which the members of the North West Company were asked to donate funds. Captain "Spanish" John McDonell wrote to his son, John McDonell "le pretre," who was at that time a partner in the North West Company, requesting a donation:

> We are building a pretty snug and decent stone Church at River aux Raisin. It is Mr. Roderick's hobby horse. It is expected to be finished this year. Mr. Roderick expects, as well as myself, that you will speak to, and encourage, such as you think proper, to assist in so pious and generous an undertaking by contributing to the completion of it.

The Mr. Roderick referred to was the Catholic missionary at St. Regis. The partners in the North West Company responded twice to the request, once in 1801 and again in 1803.

The church was constructed between 1797-1801. It is built of field stone with walls a meter thick, and measures 23 meters x 10.5 meters. The original pitched roof was altered and the bell tower removed in the late 1870s. Originally a door led from the apse to a vestry and the priest's quarters. The building served, temporarily, as a hospital during the War of 1812, and then resumed its role as a church. It became the parish hall after it was replaced by a larger church built in 1861.

To the north of the parish hall beside the Raisin River lies the old graveyard. It is here that Simon Fraser, the famous explorer, and his wife Catherine are buried. The Hudson's Bay Company erected a memorial over Fraser's grave in 1921.

After his retirement from the North West Company in 1817-18, Fraser came to St. Andrews where he had already purchased property from his brother.

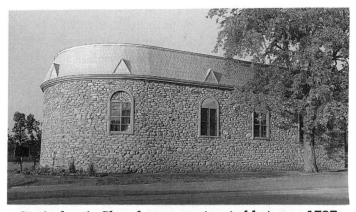

St. Andrew's Church was constructed between 1797 and 1801. When a new church was built in 1861, this building became the parish hall. Originally built with a pitch roof and bell tower, these features were removed in the 1870s. Photo by Pat MacKenna.

By late 1818 he had built a saw and grist mill. The mills do not appear to have been profitable. One story suggests that Fraser suffered heavy financial loss because the mills burned.

Fraser married Catherine MacDonell daughter of Allan MacDonell (of Leek) in 1820. She was twenty-nine and he was forty-four. They had five sons and four daughters—one daughter died in infancy.

At sixty-two years of age, Fraser, while serving with the 1st Regiment of the Stormont Militia during the Rebellions of 1837-38, fell while marching at night and suffered permanent injury to his right knee. He applied for a government pension that was granted in 1841. He then made a further unsuccessful application to the British Government for a second pension. In making his request to England, he stated that his injury had reduced "him from a state of comparative affluence to penury, owing to his not being capable to attend to his ordinary business."

Fraser died in extreme poverty at the age of eighty-six; Catherine died the following day. Some eighteen days before his death a mortgage for the sum of $1400 was taken out on his property. Very little is known about Fraser and his life at St. Andrews and no trace remains of his farm or mills. All that is visible is an Ontario Historic Sites plaque erected on land he once owned. The plaque is located 3.7 kilometers from the village. Take Highway 138 north, then turn left on Concession 6 west. Follow this road until it ends at County Road 18. The plaque is on the left.

Most of the retired fur traders were the *nouveau riche* of the era. Their ambition was to acquire the trappings of the landed gentry. Unfortunately, uncleared land in Canada at that time had little value and the government of the period did little to reward them. Consequently, Fraser, McDonell ("le pretre"), and McDonald (Gart) experienced grave financial problems in later life. Possibly the Canadian Legislature was influenced by the British Government, who tended to view these men as adventurers who had deliberately thwarted and triumphed over the charted English company of Hudson's Bay.

These men were adventurous and courageous buccaneers. Without them Canada would have remained an uncharted wilderness for years.

Directions

To return home, retrace the route to Highway 138. For those returning to Ottawa or Montreal, turn north to connect with Highway 417. For those returning to Cornwall, turn south to connect with Highway 401. Or if you wish to continue on to our next tour, make your way back to Lancaster at the junction of Highways 34 and 401.

CHAPTER 3

Glengarry Highland Roads

Preamble

Bounded on the east by the Province of Quebec, the north by Prescott County, the West by Stormont County, and the south by the St. Lawrence River where it widens into Lake St. Francis, Glengarry County is home to a unique blend of predominately Scottish, French, and English Canadians. Where else but in Glengarry County will you find a Scottish bagpiper leading the procession in a French Catholic church?

Pride in tradition runs deep in Glengarry. Emily Madsen, your host for this tour, once lived in Montreal but "fell in love with Glengarry" at first sight. A teacher, Emily came to Eastern Ontario in the late 1960s looking for an old schoolhouse to convert into her home. Instead, she purchased a weekend hobby farm near Martintown, which she subsequently moved into on a year round basis. Now teaching again, and residing with her husband in Cornwall, Emily will serve you snippets of the Glengarry "mystique" to prepare you for the day when you are ready to step out in your rented kilt for a "wee dram" with your newly found Scottish ancestors to toast the haggis being piped in on Robbie Burn's Night. Having taken this irrevocable step, you will know that you have found your own Glengarry. "Cead Mille Failte" (One Hundred Thousand Welcomes). Glengarry awaits!

I.B.

History

Glengarry County was settled in 1784 by approximately 1,000 former soldiers of the Royal Highland Emigrants (84th Regiment of Foot) and the 1st Battalion King's Royal Regiment of New York, along with their families. Glengarry is a land of big men, brave deeds, and tall tales.

Subsequently homesteaded by waves of impoverished Scottish Highlanders from 1786 to 1804 looking for a new life and the promised land, the County has been home to such Canadian legends as the Reverend John Bethune, the first Presbyterian Minister of Ontario; prospector Cariboo Cameron; John Sandfield Macdonald, the first premier of Ontario; buffalo wrestler Finnan McDonald; Lieutenant-Colonel 'Red' George Macdonnell; the fighting

GLENGARRY HIGHLAND ROADS

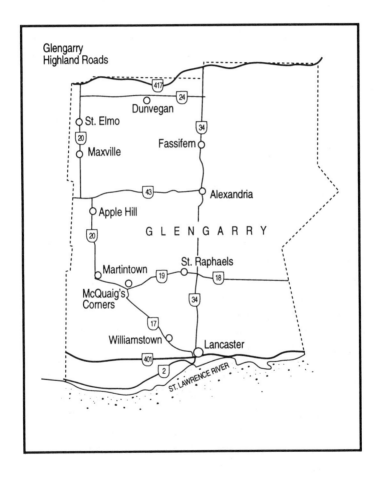

Bishop Alexander Macdonnell, and that most curious of all Canadian politicians, Prime Minister Mackenzie King, who sat for Glengarry from 1945 to 1949.

The County's heroic origins, the Highland Scot's clannishness during the formative years, along with a distinctive Gaelic language, the prominence of its citizens during Upper Canada's first years, and its relative isolation—have all led to the creation of the Glengarry "mystique."

The County was emblazoned on the Canadian psyche by early 20th century Presbyterian Minister Charles W. Gordon, known better as Ralph Connor, the author of *The Man from Glengarry* and *Glengarry School Days*, to name just two of the many books he wrote. But the county's sense of community was already well formed when he appeared.

In 1886 athlete, contractor, soldier, politician, and typical lifelong Glengarry bachelor Big Rory McLennan boasted:

> There is no county in Canada that has turned out so many successful railway men, and successful men in every walk of life, as the County of Glengarry. True, many of our young men start out in the world under many disadvantages—without a proper education, few friends, and no money. These disadvantages are got over by energy and brains, and an honest determination to reach the front ranks. Men from this county are to be met wherever you may go and as a rule you find them foremost in whatever position they have undertaken to fill (from

Royce MacGillivray and Ewan Ross, *A History of Glengarry*).

Created as a county in 1792 by Proclamation of Lieutenant-Governor Simcoe, the northern half of the original land area bordering the Ottawa River was separated from the main body to form Prescott County in 1798.

Glengarry grew steadily, and in 1891 it had 22,447 inhabitants. Subsequently, the population has declined, with only 21,164 residents counted in 1988. Glengarry has absorbed a constant influx of French Canadians from the 1860s on, so the area's lack of growth is puzzling. It seems possible that the Scots' love of adventure and travel, which took many men away, combined with the fact that around 1% of the County's young men were killed and another 4% severely injured during World War I, can account for some of the stagnation.

But tall tales abound, and adventures can be found—even if the directions are a bit confusing, as the following story shows:

Story

We were prowling the back roads in search of the site of an old still that friends had recommended as a fine spot for taking photos. Confused by a profusion of sideroads that didn't match our written directions, we stopped to show our map to an elderly man who was repairing fences at the roadside. "You'll be wanting the hermit's place over by the beaver," he said.

His muttered instructions, punctuated by long spits that held my son enthralled, left us no wiser. These included "Turn down where the old cheese factory used to be and go for—oh, I'd say, 3 to 4 miles, 'til you come to a lane. She's got a snake in her and winds a fair deal, but you can't miss her. Well, don't take this one. You want the old lane by the McKillop's place. They're all dead and gone now. Anyways, you can't miss his cabin. She's just off the end of the land, in the bush a ways, over by the beaver."

You won't be surprised to learn that we were unable to locate the site of the old still. We backtracked, however, to spend a delightful half hour with the fence repairer who was a fountain of local knowledge and was happy to explain that the beaver was a hay meadow, and the snake the grassy hump grown up between the wheel tracks of a winding country lane.

Directions

In the 1950s when I first visited Glengarry traveling west from Montreal, Highway 2 was the only route one could follow. I came to spend the summer at the Presbyterian Peace Memorial Camp near South Lancaster. Then the shoreline was natural, muddy, seemingly bottomless, and definitely fish-filled. Working farms surrounded the campgrounds, a former World War II barracks. The mysteries of country life were hinted at as we sang rousing evangelical hymns such as "Bring them in, bring them in,/Bring them in from the fields of sin . . ."

GLENGARRY HIGHLAND ROADS

And this, not far from the site of the Great Glengarry Revival of the late 19th century!

At that time, the Presbyterian Free Church by the lakeshore was crowded, night after night. Religious hysteria was rampant along with tales of miracles. Such cleansing of the "fields of sin" has not been experienced since in Glengarry. As the traveler will learn, however, much of the spirit of Glengarry, past and present, can be found in its churches.

Enter Glengarry County at the village of Lancaster, an old Loyalist settlement we toured extensively in Chapter 1 on the Perch Route. This village has a history of serving the surrounding farm population, and is now home to many former city dwellers as well. Today Lancaster welcomes visitors to craft shops and tea rooms as well as quiet, tree-lined streets. The War Memorial erected on the corner beside the Bank of Montreal attests to the memory of local heroes, including the Victoria Cross winner J.P. Nunney of World War I fame. Among the citations given him it is explained how, though wounded in two places, his section wiped out, he advanced alone carrying his own ammunition, and stopped an attack by over 200 enemies single-handedly.

Local histories tell the exploits of many former residents in all walks of life. The famed MacLennan family had a member who settled on the Island of Java on a coffee plantation after a colorful career as a fur trader. Another MacLennan was with Sherman on his "march to the sea" during the American Civil War.

After the United Empire Loyalists and the Scots, many French families came from Quebec to settle in the area, often intermingling through marriage with Catholic Scots in the area to create a special Glengarry strain. In the 1851 census of the country, 1627 are listed as residents of French origin. Many family names became anglicized as, for example, the Tyos (Taillon), the Kirkeys (Cartier), and the Droppos (Drapeau). Residents today trace their ancestry back to prominent businessmen and clerics of the 19th century such as the LeClairs of North Lancaster. Two boys who attended the brick public school in the 1920s grew up to become Jules Léger, a Governor-General of Canada, and Paul-Emile, Cardinal Léger, famous for his work in African leper colonies.

Take Highway 34, the Military Road, north through some of the oldest continuously farmed land in the province. This region has numerous bicentennial farms still operated by descendants of the original settlers. When you reach a flashing yellow light at the Brown House, site of an old inn of that name from the era of coaches, turn left to travel on Glengarry's oldest road, the King's Road, County Road 18.

The King's Road follows a continuous high stony ridge from the St. Lawrence River at Côteau du Lac to some distance west of Cornwall where it joins the Post Road. Surely it began as a much used Native trail, since most of the southern part of Lancaster Township was impassable swamp—the Sunken Township. After the War of 1812 and for the next century, the King's Road—known throughout Ontario

**Built in 1815, St. Raphael's Church was destroyed by fire in 1970. The ruins have been stabilized and a new church erected adjoining the west wing.
Photo by Pat MacKenna.**

as Dundas Street—was the main route by land from Montreal to Toronto. Besides those on the king's business, settlers used the road to get to church, grist mill, and village store. There is only local traffic now, and the small volume of it makes it difficult to imagine early days on the road.

In 1792 roads along the St. Lawrence River were largely of log construction with dangerous corduroy bridges. River travel was the preferred mode in all weather. By 1825 within Stormont, Dundas, and Glengarry, eleven two-wheeled gigs, eleven "pleasure wagons" with leather springs, and one closed carriage could be found.

Saint Raphael's Church

As you crest a rise in the King's Road, Saint Raphael's Church Ruins appear. Here is a true cradle of the Roman Catholic Church in Eastern Ontario. When this parish was founded Toronto and Ottawa were unknown, and Fort Frontenac suggested the future site of Kingston on maps of the day.

Father Alexander Macdonell (Scotus) led a group of some 500 Highlanders from Knoydart, Scotland, to North America in 1786. They left depressed economic conditions in search of greater opportunities, and suffered hardships both at sea and in their stony glens here in the new world. It is said that on their ship to Canada, the *MacDonald*, a blacksmith named McGuiness shot a seagull which fell, spattering blood on the deck. Later when the ship was in difficulty after striking a sandbar, superstitious passengers remembered the evil omen. They tied McGuiness and rushed him to the rail. But their priest Scotus ordered his release and commanded them to get down on their knees and pray to St. Raphael, saint of all travelers. The ship righted itself and the emigrants concluded the voyage safely.

The church was destroyed by fire in 1970. The ruins have been stabilized and a new church built adjoining the west wing, making for over two hundred years of continuous Roman Catholic services at St. Raphael's parish.

Across the road from the ruins is the Bishop's House, now Mount Carmel, a treatment center for alcoholics. Every July, Mount Carmel hosts a benefit concert in the church ruins. Next to the centre is Iona Academy, and by its side, Shalom, a peaceful retreat house. An historical plaque commemorates the College of Iona. The inscription reads:

> The College of Iona
> Established by the Reverend Alexander Macdonell, father of Roman Catholic education in Upper Canada and later Bishop of Kingston, the College of Iona was opened in 1826 in a log building near this site.

The central portion of the nearby stone structure, erected by Macdonell in 1808 as the presbytery for the parish, served as a residence for teachers and students. Much of the cost of construction and of the operational expenses of the school were borne by Macdonell. In addition to being the first seminary in Upper Canada, the school offered a general academic education preparing boys for secular vocations. After about ten years its functions were taken over by Regiopolis College in Kingston.

That log building at St. Raphael was, in its time, an elementary school, a chapel, and when moved to its present location on the side road leading north from the King's Road in 1914, the parish high school, and later Iona Commercial College until 1965. The offices of Maryfarm, a l'Arche community in nearby Glen Roy, are now in this venerable old building. Sit on the grassy knoll and drink in the peace of the aged and holy place. Examine the gravestones of those hardy pioneers. You're sure to come away refreshed in spirit.

John Sandfield Macdonald

As you continue west on the King's Road, another historical plaque alerts you to the birthplace of John Sandfield Macdonald, son of one of those hardy highlanders. He became one of Cornwall's most successful lawyers, founder of *The Freeholder* newspaper. From 1841 on he was elected to Parliament eight times. An eminent statesman, he was Prime Minister of what was then the Province of Canada from 1862-1864. After Confederation, which he opposed because he did not believe there were sufficient safeguards for minority rights, he became Premier of Ontario from 1867-1871. A fine statue of this Glengarrian can be found in Queen's Park in Toronto.

Fraserfield

On the King's Road west of St. Raphael's, slow down for cattle crossings and don't miss the lovingly restored log home and antique shop of Bob Gray to be found on the north side of the road. After a stop here to view reasonably priced area treasures, continue west slowly enough to appreciate the fine farm, Fraserfield, situated down in the valley to the south just before you reach McQuaig's Corners.

Colonel Alexander Fraser was an able Glengarry Militia leader, politician, and administrator. He had his manor house built of huge proportions on a 1,000 acre estate with four avenues of approach. Fraserfield's distinction lies in its sheer size, built as it was in an era when most farmers had hardly emerged from the subsistence living of pioneer times. Fraserfield has exquisite detailing, interior and exterior, from the decorative roof balustrade and dome-like cupola to the parlor fireplace adorned with six colonettes and painted to resemble polished marble. The historical value of this beautiful fieldstone house has been recognized by the Ontario Heritage Foundation, and it is being restored to its original opulence by the current owners.

Williamstown

Here at McQuaig's Corners, take County Road 27 south to the Raisin River, then turn east on County Road 17 to Williamstown along a gently curving way that hugs the river bank. This historic and picturesque village was founded in 1784 by Sir John Johnson who was granted a tract of land here by George III. Settled by both United Empire Loyalists and emigrant Scots, it was called Williamstown in honor of Sir John's father, Sir William Johnson, former Superintendent of Indian Affairs for His Majesty in the Province of New York. Intrepid French voyageurs traveled this river and named it Rivière aux Raisins because of the wild grapes that grew in abundance along the banks.

The Williamstown Fair, Ontario's oldest annual country fair, is held the second weekend in August. On land donated by Sir John, local agricultural enthusiasts show their finest, from Ayreshire cattle to zucchini loaves. Besides the games, midway, and exhibits, don't miss the concessions! Fair food is fattening but irresistible in its setting. Try the curds or the pickled cheese, the fries and fish rolls. You can get "barbe à papa," that pink candy floss confection spun around a paper cone. The best deal of the day, though, has to be the home-cooked dinner, the funds from which benefit such local groups as hockey teams and Women's Institutes. The freshest garden vegetables and fruit go into salads and pies of the first order!

The first fair on these grounds was held in 1812, the same year the building of the beautiful stone church, St. Andrew's, was begun. At the gateway to the churchyard can be found the bronze plaque to mark the founding of the first Presbyterian congregation in 1787. The indefatigable pioneer cleric Reverend John Bethune also established churches in Lancaster, Summerstown, Martintown, and Cornwall! On a typical Sunday this minister would travel many miles to deliver as many as five sermons. He baptised hundreds of settlers' children, and United Empire Loyalist descendants today proudly point to their ancestors in his church records. Stroll through the church grounds, looking at the tombstones of Williamstown's past inhabitants. The author of *Shadow of Tradition*, Carrie Holmes Macgillivray is buried here.

Story

Many of Glengarry's sons were larger than life heroes. Fur trader Big Finnan McDonald — the buffalo wrestler — was one of these "giants." Glengarry chroniclers MacGillivray and Ross relate that while on a buffalo hunt across the northwestern plains Finnan McDonald got separated from his party. Singling out a bull, he was somehow unhorsed, and attacked by it. Rather than run, Finnan grasped the bull by the horns, wrestling it to death after a struggle that lasted several hours. Never letting go, the exhausted Finnan now passed out with the horns of the bull still in his clutch. His companions later found him in this position.

At least that's the official version. Recently I was told that an eye witness to the event remembered the wrestling match somewhat differently. According to this account, the wounded bull took off after the hunting party, who reached the safety of the trees — all except poor Finnan who was tossed unmercifully by

A 1910 postcard of the Martintown covered bridge and roller mill. The bridge was replaced in the 1930s, but the mill still stands. Photo courtesy of the S.D. & G. Historical Society, Inverarden Museum (90-8.14).

the bull before he retreated. Whatever the case may be, both stories still leave Finnan's reputation as a buffalo fighter intact.

Martintown

Now retrace your steps to McQuaig's Corners. West of McQuaig's Corners, the King's Road takes you to a village that grew on the banks of the Raisin River which afforded power for grist mill and saw mill alike. Martintown originally had a covered bridge that spanned the Raisin until 1936 when the last of the wooden structures was replaced by steel and concrete. This was a thriving center in the 19th century with numerous general stores, churches, and inns. Martintown is now a quiet home for over three hundred people, ranging from retired farmers to commuters who travel as far as Ottawa and Montreal to work.

The Glengarry farmer, after clearing his land of trees, planted amid the stumps such essential crops as oats. This Scottish staple still forms a part of the diet of his descendants. Long before oat bran become a fad food, oatcakes and biscuits accompanied a hearty meal in Glengarry County. Many people here start cool days with a bowl of porridge.

One morning, an elderly Martintown man feasted on porridge his brother had thoughtfully left in a covered container in the fridge. To his chagrin, he learned later in the day that he had eaten the wallpaper paste carefully saved to complete a decorating job in progress! Now, *that's* Scots' thrift that sticks to the ribs.

The following recipe is from the *175th Anniversary Cookbook* of the United Church Women of the St. Andrew's United Church published in 1979:

> *Jean Thomson's*
> *Old Fashioned Oatcake*
>
> | | |
> |---|---|
> | 1 cup shortening | 2 cups flour |
> | 1 cup hot water | 2 cups rolled oats |
> | 1 teaspoon soda | 1/2 teaspoon salt |
> | 1/2 cup sugar | vanilla |
>
> *Mix all together – cool – roll out thin and cut in squares.*

The roots of Glengarry are in agriculture and the Martintown Mill forms an important part of that heritage. In 1971, Ian McMartin, a descendant of the founders of Martintown, purchased the now inactive grist mill. When he met an untimely death, his sister, Marjorie McMartin, gave ownership to the Raisin Region Conservation Authority. Thanks to funding by the Township of Charlottenburgh, the Ontario Heritage Foundation, and the Martintown Mill Preservation Society, the site is being preserved. The subject of landscape artists, including Peter Etril Snyder, the mill is best viewed in April when the rushing waters below are filled with spawning pickerel. And it is in early spring that the Great Raisin

The tree of life symbol is repeated on many of the gravestones in the cemetery surrounding St. Andrew's Church. Photo by Pat MacKenna.

River Canoe Race takes place. The banks near the river at Martintown offer the best sight of the bold white-water canoeists going over the dam.

St. Andrew's United Church

On the west bank south of the bridge is the Auld Kirk, St. Andrew's. Built in 1832-1836 by Presbyterians, St. Andrew's United is one of Ontario's finest rural churches. The high site overlooking the Raisin was donated by a certain Finlay McMartin. Stonemasons, whose descendants still live on the Kinloch Road (County Road 18), came out from Scotland to construct the large stone kirk to hold 800 people. After the great fire of 1906 it was reconstructed without the upper balconies. Simple yet fine decoration in wood and stencilling enhance the interior while light shining through its stained glass windows bathes the congregation in a jeweled glow. A stroll among the gravestones surrounding the church will evoke in the visitor a reverence for the rural past. One stone, that of Benjamin Clark, is shaped like a tree trunk and the tree of life symbol is repeated on many of St. Andrew's cemetery markers.

Dulwich House

Nearby on Nine Mile Road opposite Martintown Public School is an attractive 1845 late Regency cottage. The hip roof, columned veranda, floor to ceiling windows, and central doorway fitted with sidelights and a full fanlight make this a characteristic Regency Cottage. The term cottage often causes confusion, as these 1½ storey structures do not look like anything like the typical lakeside summer cottage most Canadians are familiar with. At the time that Dulwich House was built, a cottage was a 1½ storey all season home, while a Regency Villa was a two storey home. Margaret and Derek Cooper have selected and researched the interesting antiques on display. Dulwich House Antiques, which also offers Canadian arts and crafts for sale, is open year round. Please phone before visiting.

Glen Roy

Return to the mill and turn north towards Apple Hill on your Glengarry excursion. A few kilometers from Martintown you will reach a turn-off east that leads down a valley to Glen Roy. This beautiful valley is worth a side trip. Although the drive through the rolling hills of the glen can be a mite scary on a foggy evening during thaw as you dip in and out of pockets of thick mist, on a bright day you are rewarded with tranquil pastoral scenes.

It was on such a sunny afternoon that we slowed down for a great herd of black and white cows. We recognized the two young daughters of Ewen, who had just been elected President of the Glengarry Holstein Club. The red-headed girls were driving the herd home for the evening milking. Ready to razz them a little, we asked, "What kind of cows have you got there, girls?" After a moment's

Dulwich House, built in 1845. The hip roof, columned veranda, floor to ceiling windows, central doorway fitted with sidelights, and full fan light make this a characteristic Regency Cottage. Photo by Pat MacKenna.

reflection, they answered, "They're all females."

Charming farmhouses perch atop hills on both sides of the road and you will pass meandering streams and deep woods. The crossroads near the Beaudette River was once known as "Brynahoun," Gaelic for "settlement by the river." A l'Arche community, La Caravane, is housed on four properties on the northeast corner. For their attempt to live in Christian fellowship with the handicapped, the founders of this l'Arche community could not have found a more heavenly spot in 1975.

Apple Hill

Back on the paved road leading to Apple Hill, notice on your left the gravel concession roads marked I.L. for Indian Lands. Nearby is Loch Garry, which can be found by following a tortuous way east and north on these roads. At Loch Garry, there was formerly a community of general stores, a post office, and a number of families. Nathan Phillips, who later became mayor of Toronto, lived in a general store here as a child. It is now an isolated hamlet visited by summer campers, bathers, and fishermen. The Ministry of Natural Resources stocked this little lake with bass fingerlings, and the fishing might be very good still.

The best-known landmark in the village of Apple Hill is the old log building most recently operated as a blacksmith shop by Oliver Hamelin. It is a trip back in time to enter the dark depths and watch this smith toil over his hot fire in the back corner. This building is said to have been erected first in the St. Raphael's area for church services. After the construction of the stone church, this structure was moved to its present location. Imagining the great number of faithful it must have sheltered from the elements for worship, one can't help admiring the pioneer value of crowding to keep warm!

During the centennial celebrations in Apple Hill, songs were gathered from the old folk from the surrounding area that give the true festive flavor of old Glengarry. One of the best times to hear these is at the traditional post-Highland Games parties held all over the county on the August Civic Holiday weekend. The music and storytelling go on all night until revelers begin to slip away at dawn to do the morning chores. In Glengarry, people still make their own music and folks here don't keep their tongues in their pockets, keeping the oral tradition alive and well.

Maxville and the Highland Games

At Highway 43, go west the short distance to Highland Road which leads to Maxville. As you travel north to the site of the annual Highland Games, you are using an ancient route that once joined the St. Lawrence River to the Ottawa River, passing through Indian Lands. Enter the village of Maxville, named for settlers from Scotland—many of whose names began with "Mac." Year-long celebrations took place in 1991 as the village celebrated its centennial and many former townspeople returned to participate.

Maxville celebrated its Scottish heritage with the first Highland Games in 1948. With 20,000 in attendance, the Prime Minister of Canada, the Right Honorable William L. Mackenzie King, officially opened the Games. Ever since, this colorful event has been held on the first Saturday of August. There are competitions in both dancing and piping, with sports events such as caber tossing to remind us that Glengarry is the birthplace of giants!

Located at the Fair Grounds, the Glengarry Sports Hall of Fame commemorates the achievements of athletes from the County. Glengarry has produced men of great physical stature such as Big Lewis of the Alpin Grants. He is said to have once presented arms with the barrel of a cannon, and carried it on his shoulder during the military parade that followed. He felt that a musket was only a toy, not fit for a man to carry! Or consider Big Rory MacLennan, world champion at the hammer throw. This giant never again competed after 24 May 1877 when his hammer killed a child in a tragic accident. Dressed in his best to watch as an honored guest, Big Rory was persuaded to demonstrate the style that had won him such acclaim in the hammer throw. Some say that his hand caught in the chain of his watch fob, spoiling his throw. True for certain is that little Katie Kavanaugh broke away from her father, darted across the roped-off area towards her mother, and ran into the path of Big Rory's hammer. A painting of Big Rory MacLennan and a trophy won by his Tug O' War team are on display in this fascinating museum.

The Fair Grounds are also the home to the

The Maxville Highland Games are held annually on August Civic Holiday Weekend. Over 20,000 people gather annually at the Games to experience the Scottish heritage. Photo by Pat MacKenna.

Kenyon Agricultural Society's May Fair, and to an Antique Heritage Show featuring collectibles from local and outside dealers held the first Saturday in June. On Main Street, don't miss Danskin's Scottish Gift Shop which sells recordings, tartan by the meter, and supplies for dancers and pipers. There is even a Rent-a-Kilt Service for those who wish to dress suitably for social functions such as the Beaver Club Dinner or Robbie Burns' Night. When the haggis is piped into the hall, many a kilted guest rises to greet it!

Story

Maxville causes me to wonder about the very art of naming in the County of Glengarry. Nicknames often express the warm affection of family members and friends. They can also be the less charitable summing up of someone by his neighbors. Naming has been raised to a superior art here in Glengarry. Original nicknames were in Gaelic, as the following story of the Loyalists' trek from the American Colonies attests.

John MacLennan wrote in 1844 that he knew the man who was the boy of this incident. The lad's mother carried two young children on her back through the woods. In the weary journey, she thought her burden had become lighter and, sure enough, she had dropped one. She retraced her steps to find him sleeping quietly where he had fallen beside a decayed log, his hands begrimed with earth. He lived to a fine old age, well-known by the name "Spogan

Dubh" or Black-Paws, the exclamation his mother uttered upon finding him!

Because of the numerous MacDonald clan, nicknames and various spellings became the crucial elements in identifying a person. An amusing anecdote has been handed down concerning them. From the Upper Canada Regional Gazette of 26 June 1828 we learn that Alexander M'Donnel had prosecuted Alexander McDonnell for debt; that Alexander McDonnell had obtained an execution against the real estate of Alexander M'Donnell and that Angus M'Donnell, deputy sheriff of the Eastern District, had seized Alexander M'Donnell's farm in Charlottenburgh, which was sold by the high sheriff Donald M'Donnell on the 21st of July at said Donald M'Donnell's office in Cornwall . . .

Names were chosen because of physical attributes, as in Johnny Two-Thumbs, Sandy Long-Nose, Red Rory, and Black Rory, although one wonders about a blond giant of a beef farmer called Black Roddie! A habit could earn you name such as Windy, Three-Cups O' Tea, or Big Angus the Hog . . . or was the maligned Angus merely a pig farmer?

Kenny Billy Dee McLeod and his wife were known as Thunderin' Bill and Lightening Jane. Little Malcolm the Snuff, Hughie Potato John, Wooly Dunc' the Weaver, Black Allan the Dogs, Donald Big John the Pest . . . they roll off the tongue bringing a smile to the lips. To a Glengarry native, they're all in the day's news.

Highland Road Lore

As you continue north on Highland Road, notice the proud restorations of fine old homes. Many large farmhouses contain rooms of grand dimensions with high ceilings, a reaction, perhaps, to the cramped quarters of the log houses they replaced. Often they were home to extended families. Most were built around the time of Confederation when Glengarry County was experiencing a period of prosperity.

Those farmers who sold grain for export benefited from the Civil War in the United States. Higher prices for dairy products lured many into the dairy industry. Cheese factories began to grow in number, until there were 200 in Ontario in the year 1867. Labor-saving farm machinery was available now, and pride in home and family flourished.

Tales of haunting attached to some properties. While the French had their "loup garou," the Scots had the frightening "bochdan," and there has always existed in Glengarry a belief in the healing powers of a seventh son of a seventh son. A city dweller who moved into an old farmhouse told the following story.

Story

The young daughter was spending too much time shut away in her bedroom upstairs. Whenever her mother went up to fetch her in order to interest her in the goings-on that included the rest of the family, the mother had the distinct impression that she was interrupting something. Often a conversation seemed to stop just as she set foot on the top stair. She took to using different staircases (there were three!) and stepping as softly as possible. She eventually heard the child talking at great length and with great animation. The child finally admitted that she talked to "the gramma that comes to see me." The family assumed she was having trouble adjusting to the lonelier life in the country and had invented a companion. Later, neighbors told this tale of their haunted house.

The last member of the family that had built the house lived in it to a ripe old age. The elderly lady, much loved by all, was visited regularly by relatives. It was during one such visit that the tragedy occurred. The woman's grandchild drowned in the well, and she herself died soon after in great sorrow. She became a rather benevolent ghost, only visiting little children.

St. Elmo

North of Maxville at St. Elmo are two historical markers, one at the log Congregational Church, and the other at the brick Presbyterian Church. This is the birthplace of renowned Canadian writer Charles W. Gordon. Using the pen name Ralph Connor, this writer drew material from his early childhood (1860-1871) in the manse of the Presbyterian Free Church at St. Elmo to write his famous Glengarry books. He attended the log school at nearby Athol, learning farming and forestry skills that were so much a part of life in his day. Many still find *The Man from*

Glengarry a rollicking good read today, steeped as it is in the legend and the mystique of the County.

Dunvegan

Follow the sign on Highland Road that leads you east onto the road to Dunvegan, Gaelic for "little fort." There you will find the Star Inn and Local History Building, perhaps the finest small museum in Ontario. This thirty-year old museum complex includes a log inn, with the original 1840 bar and tap room, now turned officially dry.

The locals, with good Scottish sense, managed the best of both worlds in the tap-room that served "Pipperment Ginger Cinanamon and Lemond Syrup" to the righteous and a wee dram from the trapdoor behind the bar to the less strong-willed. The Museum houses a collection assembled and curated by the Glengarry Historical Society, and the Scottish heritage is dominant. The collection highlights bagpipes, Gaelic writings, and the legendary cast iron pot from which Bonnie Prince Charlie himself is said to have shared a meal over in Glen Morriston during the Troubles. At the Annual Book Fair, held on the third weekend in July by the Glengarry Historical Society, you might find treasures such as out-of-print editions of some of Glengarry's famous authors. Gaelic Bibles and the complete works of Ralph Connor are on display. In the Reference Room Archives much of the history of the County can be traced. In the livery shed are farm implements and sleighs. The barn contains a collection of tools, and the loft is set up as an early textile center. A miniature cheese factory with authentic equipment goes into production on occasion, to the delight of locals as well as visitors. Stop at a picnic table for a rest, and drink in the atmosphere of this pioneer setting along with refreshments from the summer tearoom.

Kirkhill

Continue along the Dunvegan Road to Highway 34 where you can turn south towards Alexandria. At Laggan, a detour east will take you to Kirkhill, or Glenleg as it was once known. This corner was once a prosperous spot at the time the stage coach went by here. Now the shadow of the past is cast only by the two Protestant churches, St. Columba and Kirkhill United. Farther on this road toward Dalkeith don't miss the cairn and plaque erected by the Clan McLeod Society of Glengarry to honor their ancestors, the settlers who came in 1794.

Fassifern

Back on Highway 34 turn south and drive past Fassifern, which ranks as a beautifully named hamlet along with Lochinvar, MacCrimmon, Brodie, Breadalbane, Lochiel, Glen Nevis, and Skye, especially sweet-sounding off the lips of a Glengarry highlander. These hamlets, prosperous in early days, withered with the advent of the railway and automobile. This is clearly suggested by their Post Office closings:

The Star Inn and Local History Building, Glengarry Museum, Dunvegan, was built in 1840. It is perhaps the finest small museum in Ontario.
Photo by Pat MacKenna.

Breadalbane (1916), Brodie (1915), Fassifern (1915), Glen Nevis (1914), Kirkhill (1928), Lochiel (1914), Lochinvar (1890), MacCrimmon (1919), and Skye (1915). Glengarrians turn out in the hundreds to battle the continued assault on rural post offices, which are as important today in the social life of the county as they were in earlier days.

Alexandria

You are now nearing the "Hub of Glengarry," Alexandria. The disbanded regiment of the Glengarry Fencibles, accompanied by their chaplain, Father Alexander Macdonnell, settled here in 1803. One of the first buildings erected was the grist mill, giving the place its first name of Priest's Mills, later changed to Alexandria in honor of its founder. The mill pond, once boggy and weedy, is now a lake surrounded by an attractive park.

A church was first built on the site of the present St. Finnan's in 1833. Described as the richest parish in the Diocese of Kingston in 1882, the present Cathedral was erected in 1884-85. Five years later the Diocese of Alexandria was formed. And a decade later the Bishop's Palace was built. This building served as the diocesan headquarters until it was moved to Cornwall in 1971. In 1976 St. Finnan's became co-cathedral with the Church of the Nativity of the Blessed Virgin Mary in Cornwall for the newly created Diocese of Alexandria-Cornwall. The old Palace was sold in 1976, and is now a seniors' residence.

Displaying a heightened sense of Glengarry pride, authors Royce MacGillivray and Ewan Ross in their *History of Glengarry* note that the last four Bishops were 'imports,' leading these two historians to question, "Has the quality of the people we produce dropped off or is it the hybrid nature of our Scottish-French Catholicism at fault when outside men are needed for Bishops?". As for the town, it became an incorporated village in 1884, and a town in 1903. In 1911 it had a population of 2,323; today it numbers 3,314.

Alexandria is the commercial and cultural center of the area, featuring such well-known businesses as Harriet MacKinnon's Glengarry Bookstore at 45 Main Street South. This store stocks an excellent collection of local histories, geneological works, and historical fiction related to the United Counties. And as you near the end of a day's rambling through Glengarry County, pause to consider what flavors life today in this area. A recent copy of *The Glengarry News*, printed weekly in Alexandria, can help you do just that. Visit *The News* offices on Main Street opposite Mill Square during business hours or buy the paper at stores throughout the county. Celebrating its centennial in 1992, *The Glengarry News* flourishes today recording events and sustaining culture — and winning awards doing it. Angus H. McDonnell wrote for the *News* from the time he was a teenager. He began by writing obituaries, one or two a month when on holiday from school, progressed to sports reporting, and was still composing a weekly column at the age of more than eighty! As curator of the Glengarry Sports Hall of Fame, Angus

A 1920 photograph of the Bishop's House, Alexandria. Photo courtesy of the S.D. & G. Historical Society, Inverarden Museum (88-5.36).

Houi McDonnell impressed all with his love for his people and his homeland. Fittingly, he was the only sports hero inducted into the Hall in 1992, the year of his death.

Mill Square is situated at the center of the town, but the old mill is, unfortunately, empty.

Glengarry Accommodations

If this visit sparks a desire to learn more about Glengarry, stay a while in one of the excellent Bed and Breakfast accommodations offered in the County.

Guelda and Robert McRae welcome overnight guests at MacPine Farms on the south service road of the 401, about one kilometer east of the Lancaster exit. Enjoy their century old home, shaded by large old pine trees. It's only a five minute walk down a farm lane to their cottage by the lake where you can swim, fish, boat, or just relax and watch the ships go by on the Seaway.

In Lancaster village, turn west on Pine Street on the road to Williamstown and you will find Bed and Breakfast Country Style about three kilometers along. Tasteful renovations have been made to this red-roofed century home which sits on ten acres by the river bank. Marjorie and Malcolm Highet are old hands at Bed and Breakfast, having first welcomed visitors during Expo '67 to their Pointe Claire home. They themselves have stayed at Bed and Breakfasts from Europe to New Zealand. Have a swim in the pool before you tackle a hearty English breakfast and a day's touring from this well-located home base. Be sure to get back for tea at four!

Cead Mille Failte
(One Hundred Thousand Welcomes)

Glengarry welcomes you warmly. Drive out to attend the many annual events, and to see the sites and villages missed on this day trip. If you are an armchair traveler, try reading the many books written about this area. Arrange a subscription to *The Glengarry News*. Whatever you do, I know you'll want to keep in touch with the spirit of Glengarry County, a deeply-rooted part of the Canadian family tree.

Directions

To return to Ottawa or Montreal, follow Highway 34 north from Alexandria to Highway 417. To return to Cornwall, take Highway 34 south to Highway 401. Our next tour begins in the "Seaway City" of Cornwall, the county seat for the United Counties of Stormont, Dundas, and Glengarry.

CHAPTER 4

Touring Cornwall

Preamble

Slightly more than an hour's drive from Montreal to the east, Ottawa to the north, and a little under two hours from Kingston to the west, Cornwall was first pioneered by United Empire Loyalists in 1784, making it one of Ontario's first European settlements. The town soon became an administrative center for the United Counties of Stormont, Dundas, and Glengarry, with headquarters in the County Courthouse and Jail, erected in 1833. Located on the St. Lawrence River, Cornwall grew to be an important market town, then an industrial center with the development of water power from the Cornwall Canal, a little less than a century after its founding. French Canadians from western Quebec flocked into the town, transforming Cornwall into a bilingual community. In 1959 the city changed focus again with the completion of the St. Lawrence Seaway and

Hydro Power Project, signalling the beginning of modern Cornwall.

Today the remnants of Loyalist, Victorian, waterfront, industrial, and multicultural Cornwall are everywhere to be found. Long time resident Eileen Cunningham takes us back to the days when the steamers from around the world passed through the canal which ran beside Water Street. She introduces us to the city with a tour north up Pitt Street past the art gallery, bakery, and bookshop, before turning west to visit the United Counties Museum. We then travel east along Montreal Road to "Le Village," the center of the French community, and finally return to the waterfront development in Lamoureux Park, presided over by the clocktower and designed to give Cornwall residents and visitors a sense of the historic past and promising future of this city on the river.

I.B.

History

Cornwall's history has always been tied to the river. The Mohawks came here from their valley in the south every summer to fish. The voyageurs named the rapids in the river near the present town of Cornwall Pointe Maligne. Much altered, the Point is still part of present-day Cornwall. Located in Lamoureux Park, in the now-tamed St. Lawrence, it is accessible by a boat ramp.

The town was not permanently settled until 1784

TOURING CORNWALL

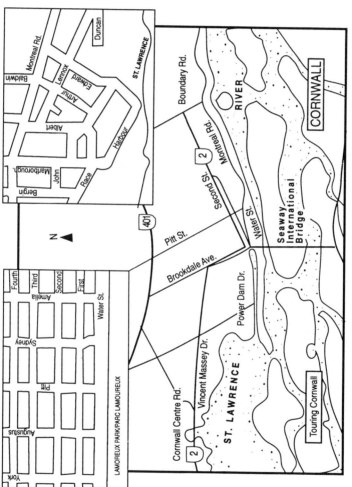

City maps courtesy Heritage Cornwall.

when the European, American, and Native United Empire Loyalists arrived at this frontier outpost under the protection of Sir John Johnson, leader of the King's Royal Regiment of New York. Initially, this garrison town was named New Johnstown in his honor, but the name was later changed to Cornwall. In 1803 the Reverend John Strachan opened Cornwall Grammar School for boys. Many of Canada's future leaders received their secondary education at this institution which is perpetuated as Cornwall Collegiate Institute and Vocational School.

At first not much more than a grouping of farms, the town evolved into the administrative seat of the United Counties with the construction of the Court House and Gaol in 1833. The completion of the 20 kilometer Cornwall Canal in 1843, the last link in the water transportation route between Montreal and Toronto, gave rise to further expansion. In 1850 the town numbered 1,646 people: 1,137 born in Canada, 377 Irish-Americans—who had probably been employed working on the canal—and 132 French Canadians.

Eventually the canal's water power was harnessed for industrial development, providing the impetus that transformed Cornwall from an agricultural center to a factory town. The water rights to the canal were used to power the machinery of textile and paper mills. These industries established the industrial base on which entrepreneurs could build. Cornwall's natural resources alone could not have guaranteed continued growth, however. The town was fortunate to have a forward-looking Town Council which valued enterprise. On 9 February

1871 the councilors moved:

> this Municipal Council, duly recognizing the importance of manufactories in this country and that such add considerably to the welfare of the community in this country and that such add considerably to the welfare of the community where [they are] established, pledge themselves to aid and assist all cotton, woollen and other similar factories which may be . . . established within this municipality.

Cornwall the factory town had been born.

This favorable civic reception persuaded businessmen from Montreal to invest in Cornwall. In 1872 the Canada Cotton Mill was built and in 1882 it became the first industrial building in Ontario to be illuminated by electric lights designed by Thomas Edison.

Now boasting three new factories built in four years when the rest of the country was suffering from a recession, the town's population increased from 2,033 in 1871 to 4,468 in 1881. Initially staffed by some 400 workers of Scottish descent, these factories acted as a magnet to the laboring community in Quebec, laying the basis for Cornwall's modern bilingual culture. Not only did the population double in this ten year period, but the French—numbering 1,323 and located in the east end—became the largest ethnic group in town. For many years Cornwall was divided along Marlborough Street, with the French-speaking population to the east, and the English-speaking population to the west. Today the French downtown, known as "Le Village," is still in the east end along Montreal Road, while the main downtown runs from the Cornwall Square north along Pitt Street to Third Street. Industrialization not only altered the rural nature of the town forever, it also spelled the beginning of the end of the Loyalist dominance of local affairs, as Catholics now outnumbered Protestants 2,290 to 2,183.

In 1924 another major industry, British-owned Courtauld's viscose rayon plant, located in Cornwall. Starting with a staff of 100, it employed 1,753 by 1936, in the midst of the Great Depression.

In 1934 Cornwall celebrated the centennial of its incorporation as a town with the official opening of the Roosevelt International Bridge. The town prospered through the war years and in the 1950s attention was once again focused on the St. Lawrence River. Efforts to harness its power culminated in 1959 with the completion of the St. Lawrence Seaway and the Hydro Power Project. The face of Cornwall was changed forever. When the building of the St. Lawrence Seaway was announced, it appeared as if the city would continue to grow. This optimism proved to be unjustified; when the Seaway was completed one local industry after another closed down, throwing over 1,700 people out of work in the textile trade alone. Altogether 3,260 people were put on welfare, causing the Federal Government to label the city "Depressed." The situation would have been disastrous if it hadn't been for the emergence of Domtar Fine Papers (opened in 1883 as the Toronto Manufacturing Company) as the

Exhibitors prepare to greet more than 10,000 visitors to the Cornwall Civic Complex during the annual Fall Home and Trade Show. Photo courtesy of the Cornwall Chamber of Commerce.

town's largest employer. In 1960 Domtar expanded with the installation of paper Machine No. 6, capable of producing 40,000 tons of paper a year, and in 1966 this advance was followed by the addition of Machine No. 7. The city's situation was also saved by Cornwall Industrial Development Limited, created in 1959 with entrepreneurial and municipal help. By 1965, C.I.D.L. had filled the empty cotton mills with various industries and attracted 1,500 jobs.

Despite this and similar initiatives that have given the city most of the amenities of larger centers, it retains charm, informality, and a relaxed pace.

The Cornwall Canal Park System

Located on the south side of Water Street, Lamoureux Park was named in honor of Lucien Lamoureux, Cornwall's M.P. for twelve years, Speaker of the House of Commons, and later Ambassador to Belgium and Luxembourg. It is a popular place in summer, especially on Canada Day when Cornwall's citizens turn out for day-long picnics and games, culminating in spectacular fireworks at dark.

An historic clocktower serves as the entrance to the park. The design is based on the old city post office clocktower and uses the old clock's faces with the latest time keeping mechanisms to keep it accurate! The original inner works, along with a heritage display, are around the base. Since the tower is Victorian, the clock started keeping time again on Victoria Day 1992.

TOURING CORNWALL

The Civic Complex, situated in the park on landfill, is the hub of many city activities. It houses the Backstage restaurant and lounge, a convention center, and the Ed Lumley arena, named for the mayor of Cornwall who was later M.P. for Stormont-Dundas for much of the 1970s, Minister of Trade and Commerce, and then Minister of Communications and Culture. The arena was also the home of the Cornwall Royals hockey team, winners of the Memorial Cup in 1972, 1980, and 1981. The arena served as the forum for a World Junior Hockey Tournament graced by the presence of Wayne Gretsky, and has been used to stage the World Junior Curling Championships and Skate Canada.

Memorable concerts have been given in the arena by Count Basie, Anne Murray, and the Irish Rovers, among others. Cornwall has enjoyed international dog shows and Royal Lippizan stallions. The Huron Hockey school is a yearly occurrence, and of course the world comes to Cornwall for Worldfest/Festimonde.

Designed for use by the general public, the Complex fulfils that role superbly. It has housed craft, home, and trade shows. Health-conscious citizens use the indoor promenade for exercise programs. The participants range in age from young sprinters to seniors pursuing an active lifestyle protected from the vagaries of weather. Six times around the arena is a mile and you can go at your own pace on an excellent surface with a view of the St. Lawrence River. Don't forget to bring your sneakers when you come to visit.

Sammy in the Sunlight, Cornwall Canal.

**The original "Seaway Sammy" and his friends swimming in the old Cornwall Canal, with the former Roosevelt Bridge in the background.
Photo courtesy S.D. & G. Historical Society, Inverarden Museum (86-19. 15).**

To the east of the complex is Marina 200, with 160 boat slips, 70 set aside for visitors. You might want to take a stroll to view the imposing building across Water Street at Amelia. It's the Lionel Chevrier Building, named for the M.P. for Stormont from 1935-54, Minister of Transport in 1945, and President of the St. Lawrence Seaway Authority 1954-58.

On the west side of the complex, at the Lion's Club Bandshell, you can hear music ranging from ethnic to bluegrass on most summer evenings. You can walk the paths beside the river or follow the bicycle path to Guindon Park for 20 kilometers of beautiful scenery with picnic tables and washrooms along the way.

In the park near the foot of York Street, the Canada Cottons Stormont Mill used to be situated on the river bank, and to the west a house was built for the canal superintendent in 1872. The mill closed down in 1959 and burned in a spectacular Hallowe'en night fire two years later. When the canal closed the superintendent's house was no longer needed and it was sold to the local wing of The Royal Canadian Air Force Association. It is easily identified today by the Canadian 347 training plane mounted outside.

Bicycle and walking paths beyond the lush lawns off Lamoureux Park wind along what remains of the Cornwall canal and lead to fishing spots and more lovely scenery. There is an old set of steps leading into the water on the north bank of the canal. Steps used to exist at regular intervals along the canal and were great places to congregate on summer evenings. Many a Cornwallite learned to swim holding on to a bottom step under the watchful eyes of their elders.

Behind Domtar is an abandoned lock, once busy with canal traffic, now picturesque with wildflowers rampant around the weathered wood. A short distance farther along you can see the pylons from the old Roosevelt Bridge in the river, and nearby, under swiftly flowing water, a large wheel. Going into the water upstream and floating face down with eyes wide open to see the wheel, which seemed like an underwater monster waving its tentacles, was a daily ritual for youngsters in the 1930s. They took the wheel for granted and never questioned where it came from.

This wheel is a remnant of the Cornwall Bridge, predecessor to the Roosevelt. During construction of the Cornwall Bridge in 1898 a pier on the south span collapsed, claiming 15 lives. Disaster struck for a second time on 23 June 1908 when pier nine, supporting the swing wheel gave way, and the wheel, plummeted into the river. The sunken wheel, which has piqued the curiosity of children for decades, is a monument to all the lives that were lost building the forerunners of the Seaway International Bridge, the easy avenue to the United States that we take for granted today.

After the Chevrier Locks were installed, the new International bridge was given a 36.6 meter (120 foot) clearance to admit the passage of sea-going vessels. Overall the north span of the bridge, opened in 1962, is 1,624.8 meters long ending on Cornwall Island. It is necessary to take a second shorter bridge to enter the U.S.A.

An aerial photograph of Cornwall's two International Bridges. Cornwall Island is in the center, with Canada Customs in the middle. The new Seaway International Bridge is on the right. Photo courtesy S.D. & G. Historical Society, Inverarden Museum.

Continuing farther west, one comes to the Moses-Saunders International Hydro-Electric Power Dam, the world's first International Power Dam. The Powerhouse is comprised of two identical components. Overall it is 1,006 meters long, 49 meters high and has 32 generators with an installed capacity of 1,800 megawatts. The headpond holds approximately 23 billion cubic feet of water. The dyke winds for some 5.5 kilometers and is made of 5 million cubic yards of glacial till. The headpond funnels 55 million gallons of water per minute down a 29 meter drop to power 16 Canadian turbines generating 7.1 terrawatt hours of energy into the Ontario Hydro grid system.

There are two 33 meter high abutments in the dyke, following the old Cornwall canal channel, large enough to accept a full seaway-size channel at a later date. According to Lionel Chevrier in his book about the project, "They served to protect Canada's right to build duplicate facilities on our side as and when the Canadian Government so decided."

Tours of the R.H. Saunders Energy Information Center atop the dam include an audio-visual presentation of the construction of the St. Lawrence Seaway, a look at a working scale model of the station, and other interesting displays. Located at the end of Second Street West, the center is open daily throughout the summer and is wheelchair accessible. Picnic tables, washrooms, and plenty of parking make it a convenient place to bring the whole family.

The bicycle path just east of the dam leads to Guindon Park comprised of 500 acres of former

This 1958 photo shows the removal of the cofferdam in front of the Moses-Saunders International Hydro-Electric Dam, Cornwall, June 1958. Photo courtesy of the Power Authority of the State of New York.

Loyalist land in the west end of Cornwall. Development was begun and the land was transformed into a recreational area, named Guindon Park to honor M.P.P. Fern Guindon.

The bicycle path makes the park a natural rest stop for cyclists on their way to and from the Long Sault Parkway. There are plenty of secluded spots for picnics in the summer, and in winter the park is alive with cross country skiers on well laid out trails. The pond, which is charming in summer and full of wildlife, becomes a skating rink with a slide ramp for sleds nearby in winter. A pocket in a pine wood has been carved out for a smaller rink where trees protect skaters from the wind. There is a seasonal sleigh ride program on Sundays. The park boasts a boat ramp, and on a recent lunch break there I saw two hikers cooling their feet in the river while Canada geese swam by with their downy babies in tow.

The bicycle path continues on from Guindon Park to the island causeways of the Long Sault Parkway.

Story

The following tale was first told in the Canadian Illustrated News, *26 January 1878. Since then Cornwall residents have often boasted of catching elephant-sized fish in the river.*

Learning that the circus was coming to town a group of Cornwall boys raised $100.^{00} to persuade the circus manager to let his elephant swim the St. Lawrence. After much pushing and shoving the *elephant entered the River making straight for the south shore. In the words of one of the boys everyone now headed for all available rowboats "to turn the huge beast back." One of the participants recounted that "they might as well have attempted to stop an iceberg. Mr. Elephant was bound for the south shore and he pushed obstructing boats away as though they were so many straws." Reaching dry land, it took everyone's persuasive abilities to coax the elephant back across the River forcing the paying show to be cancelled here and in nearby Prescott.*

Not wanting to risk Cornwall again, the circus manager planned not to stop here on his next tour, and to go through the town at night. Not to be cheated out of their fun, the boys planned a trap. Knowing that elephants enjoy potatoes, and learning the circus' timetable, they scattered potatoes along the route the circus would pass while sneaking through. Achieving complete surprise the cavalcade was suddenly halted at 2 a.m. when the elephant found his first treat. Intent on enjoying every last morsel the elephant zig-zagged thought the streets of Cornwall until the sun rose giving the town a free show.

Ivy Hall and the Earthquake

If you retrace your steps back to Lamoureux Park, you will find yourself at the corner of York Street and Water Street, facing a solid brick building with an early street marker still attached. Purchased in 1851 by John Sandfield Macdonald, Ontario's first premier, the building became known as Ivy Hall

A 1947 photograph of the old Hotel Dieu Hospital, founded in 1897 by Sister Janet Macdonell. Photo courtesy S.D. & G. Historical Society, Inverarden Museum.

when the Fourth Battalion placed the roman numerals IV over the door while they were billeted there. In 1898 it became the Hotel Dieu, Cornwall's first hospital. In 1955, with the original Ivy Hall building gone the hospital moved to larger quarters on McConnell Avenue, and the remaining old building was renamed MacDonell Memorial in memory of Sister Janet MacDonell, one of the Religious Hospitallers of St. Joseph who operated the Hotel Dieu. The Mac, as it was fondly known, eventually moved to join the new Hotel Dieu as the Janet MacDonell Pavilion, and Ivy Hall was vacant once again.

The next phase in its long history has seen the building converted to apartments for seniors with a physical connection to St. Joseph's Villa Nursing Home located on York Street.

Imagination could conjure up scenes of dashing officers and ladies in ball gowns arriving for lavish entertainments to the skirl of bagpipes in Ivy Hall's heyday.

But there are other, more dramatic memories associated with Ivy Hall.

Story

One late summer evening in 1944, glass globes atop the tall light standards by the front door crashed to the ground of Ivy Hall. Plaster fell inside the building and the resulting dust resembled smoke. Someone started screaming "Fire!" Cornwall was experiencing the terrifying earthquake of 4 September 1944.

Just after midnight, within the space of a few minutes, there were four tremors which caused severe damage to the town's churches, homes, and industries. The Roosevelt International Bridge was damaged, and the smoke stack at the Howard Smith paper mill split. Shocked residents rushed into the streets in nightclothes. Aftershocks kept everyone on edge and it was days before the extent of the damage to Cornwall was known. We have had other quakes since, but none have surpassed the intensity or topped the memory of the earthquake of 1944.

The District Court House and Gaol

A stroll further east along Water Street brings you to the District Court House and Gaol (70 Water Street West).

The District Court House and Gaol, officially opened in 1833, is one of the oldest surviving judicial structures in Ontario still in use. Constructed of dressed limestone in the neo-classic style, it is situated on the northwest corner of Pitt and Water Streets with its cannons facing the St. Lawrence River.

Despite its staid appearance, it has a colorful past, having housed a good share of murderers, and having lost an embarrassing number of escapees. In 1866, six alleged Fenians awaiting trial tunneled under the Gaol's stone wall and escaped to a waiting boat in the river. They fled to the United States during a thunderstorm. In 1976 an agile prisoner scaled the Gaol wall and left on a convenient motorcycle.

The District Court House and Gaol. The limestone neo-classic core was constructed in 1833, the brick wing on the right was added in 1885. There is a dungeon; currently it is used to store potatoes. Photo courtesy S.D. & G. Historical Society, Inverarden Museum.

Cornwall's last hanging was scheduled for 19 January 1954, but the convicted man escaped the hangman in a very final way—he swallowed cyanide an hour before the execution was to take place.

Some remember the Court House in the days when there were still horsedrawn vehicles on Cornwall's streets. There was a fountain on Water Street, donated by the Women's Christian Temperance Union in memory of Judge Jacob Farrand Pringle, 1816-1901, an historian and author of *Lunenburg or the Old Eastern District*. It was not uncommon as late as the 1930s to see someone having a drink at the fountain while a horse was imbibing from the water trough on the other side.

This was one of four public drinking fountains constructed locally by the Women's Christian Temperance Union. The fountains were found throughout the province; women hoped that if men could drink free, refreshing water, they would not consume alcoholic beverages.

The women sang:

We women pray for better times,
And work right hard to make 'em;
You men vote liquor with its crimes,
And we just have to take em!

The view from the Court House has changed since then. The canal is no longer on the other side of Water Street with boats tied to stanchions near the Canada Steamship Line warehouses. The swing bridge at the foot of Augustus Street is just a memory, but we have in their place a lovely waterfront park created by the reclamation of canal lands.

The Cornwall Regional Art Gallery

A walk up Pitt Street will take you to the Cornwall Regional Art Gallery. The Cornwall Gallery Society (incorporated in 1980) organized exhibitions in borrowed museum and library space for two years until it became apparent that a more permanent location was needed. The Regional Art Gallery came into being with help from the Cornwall Arts Development Committee and a loyal corps of volunteers. The first show, "Cornwall Through the Eyes of An Artist," was opened in the Gallery's new 500 square foot space at 107 Pitt Street in 1982. Soon outgrowing this locale, it moved to its present location at 164 Pitt Street in 1986. The tenth anniversary was recently marked with "A Visual Celebration" by artists who participated in the original show. A second display, "Canada and What It Means To Be a Canadian," by some of the Gallery's regular artists was registered with the Canada 125 Committee and is the subject of a commemorative brochure. CRAG, as it is affectionately known, is a vital focus for community arts and fine crafts. A Gallery Shoppe offers the wares of local artisans.

The Sanctuary

There is a stationer's shop at 217 Pitt Street that has served Cornwall since 1899 when Charles W. Kyte founded the business. Reginald Kyte purchased the shop from his father in 1939 and operated it successfully for forty-nine years.

Kyte's will always be associated in my mind with a leaky pen. In the 1930s, a time of utilitarian navy or black fountain pens, I discovered a powder blue one in their showcase. I immediately began to covet that pen. I paid a daily visit to make sure it was still in its place while I scrounged the price of ownership. With the money in nickels and dimes, I entered the shop to find it gone. I was told it was found to be defective and removed from the stock. I pleaded to buy it anyway but was told firmly, "We do not deal in shoddy goods."

My cloud had a silver lining. A week later when I went to the store to pick up a music book ordered for me, Mr. Kyte wrapped the book in brown paper and tied it neatly with string. When the tedious musical exercises were unwrapped, there between the middle pages was my pen. Reginald Kyte was right. It leaked, but I happily went on to bigger and better blots in my copy book to the despair of my teachers. It was not until I was older that I appreciated the values that would not let a man make a profit on a faulty pen but gave him too much heart to disappoint a child.

The store was sold to Joan and Jack Earle in 1988 and the Kyte name was retired, but not its traditions. The store's unique tin ceiling from old ice cream parlor days, original glass fronted counters, and period light fixtures make it a wonderful place to browse. It is still a family business. Now known as the Sanctuary it is Cornwall's last independent book store. You can buy flags, religious literature, art supplies, nautical charts, topographic maps, and books of all kinds, including those of local authors, and I must not forget to mention... pens that do not leak.

Riley's Bakery

I remember a man in a bake shop on lower Pitt Street in the 1930s who said his name was Jimmy Cinnamon. I went there every Saturday morning with the nickel my grandmother gave me for being a perfect child. While I went through the painful process of choosing an eccles cake, Jimmy Cinnamon waited patiently. It was difficult because the cakes were not uniform in size and getting the most for your money was important at that time. The difficulty was compounded by the fact that a number of my cronies were also making choices and the jockeying for position was strenuous. Jimmy Cinnamon produced a clean cloth and whistled cheerfully as he wiped nose marks from the front of his glass showcase when we left en masse.

We did not go far, just to the curb in front of the shop. We all had our reasons for stopping there. Some were afraid their gooey confections would not travel well, others were not supposed to be eating between meals, and of course my own reason was a compelling one. I was in danger of meeting ravenous cousins on the way home and family rules would have forced me to share. One eccles cake does not go far. We sat with our legs dangling in the dust of Pitt Street, devoured our treats, licked our fingers, and formed enduring friendships.

For years doubters have been telling me that the man in the bake shop was pulling our legs about his name and my grandmother was doing the same with her perfect child story. As Jimmy Cinnamon seems an improbable name for a baker, I too had begun to doubt. But I have found a new Jimmy Cinnamon— his name is Rob Curran, and he and his wife Anne preside over Riley's Bakery at 248 Pitt Street. The bakery was owned and operated by the Riley family for years, and at one time it had a machine which turned out a steady procession of old fashioned cake doughnuts. Passing pedestrians were fascinated as they watched at the window, and it required a strong will to pass on without buying at least one or two.

The Currans have a glass-fronted showcase too, and I still have a problem with decisions when I stand in front of it. There are delicious turnovers with ample fillings of apple, cherry, raspberry or strawberry, sugar cookies, tender crusted pies, plump loaves of bread, and crusty rolls. I don't leave nose marks on the glass anymore, but when I leave with a sugary pecan loaf in a white box tied with string, I hanker to sit on a curb.

I learned recently that there was a bake shop at 49 Pitt Street in 1933-34. The baker was James Cinnamond. I feel a great sense of vindication. If Jimmy Cinnamon was real, it is quite possible that

The Capitol Theater's "Spanish Courtyard" auditorium in 1947. The theater opened 23 January 1928 to a capacity crowd of 1,321. The theater was leveled in 1991 despite nation-wide attempts to preserve it. Photo courtesy of the Ontario Archives (RG. 56, C-4).

my grandmother was correct and I really was a perfect child. It seems logical to me!

The Capitol Theater

Walk north on Pitt Street, away from the water, and turn left on Second Street. On the north side of the street is the site of the once famous Capitol Theater.

The Capitol opened on 23 January 1928 to a capacity crowd of 1,321. Built during a period that valued elegance and glamor, the Capitol's exterior, in the restrained neoclassic style, belied the extravagance within. The opening night audience was entertained by the music of Jerome Kern, played by the Capitol's five piece orchestra, before being given a tour of the theater. The Greek Revival plaster mouldings, pilasters, scrolls, and brass railings elicited comment and the audience was left in awe of the Spanish Courtyard auditorium.

To create the courtyard, the auditorium's ceiling was used as a screen onto which a hidden projector played stars, clouds, and other effects to suggest an open sky. To complete the courtyard, the walls were elaborately decorated with plaster columns, cornices, fans, and galleries to give the impression the theater really was enclosed by a garden wall.

Allied with Famous Players in 1929, the Capitol became the 10th theater in Ontario to be equipped with a sound system. Five years later the Capitol's sky was turned off. Tastes changed, large theaters became obsolete, and the Capitol closed in 1977. Purchased by the Save the Capitol Committee, it reopened in 1978 and in 1979 was declared an historic building by City Council.

Seven years later the Committee declared bankruptcy and the theater closed again. The theater was again threatened with demolition and in 1990 the Capitol Action Group formed to fight its destruction; despite these efforts City Council ordered the theater levelled in 1991.

Other Historical and Cultural Sites

Trinity Anglican Church (105 Second Street West) was built to replace an earlier wood frame building that had been constructed for the Reverend John Strachan. Begun in 1869, the addition of a steeple in 1987 completed the building. In the cemetery adjacent to the church the earliest tombstone dates back to 1789.

The Stormont Row Housing (York and 1st Streets) is an example of industrial row housing erected in 1881 for employees of the Stormont Cotton Mill.

John Chesley's Inn (40 First Street West) was built in the 1820s as a stagehouse for John Chesley. The Georgian style architecture is evident in the symmetrical facade.

Festivities at the time of the first sod turning for the Cornwall Canal were held here in 1834. The front door is said to have come from John Sandfield Macdonald's home at Ivy Hall when it was demolished in the 1920s. While Chesley's may have been *the* Cornwall Inn, it appears that some travelers found it somewhat lacking. Mrs. William Radcliff in 1832 wrote that it "is a wretched place; bad attendance, worse rooms, ill furnished; vile beds and no rest." These sentiments were echoed by no less an authority than the godmother of Canadiana, Catharine Parr Traill who complained,

> We had some difficulty in obtaining a lodging, the inns being full of travellers; here, for the first time, we experienced something of that odious manner ascribed, though doubtless too generally, to the American tavern-keeper. Our host seemed perfectly indifferent as to the comfort of his guests, leaving them to wait on themselves or go without what they wanted. The absence of females in these establishments is a great drawback where ladies are travelling. The women keep entirely out of sight, or treat you with that offensive coldness and indifference that you derive little satisfaction from . . . After some difficulty in obtaining sight of the landlady of the inn . . . and asking her to show me a chamber where we might pass the night, with a most ungracious air she pointed to a door which opened into a mere closet, in which was a bed divested of curtains, one chair, and an apology for a wash-stand. Seeing me in some dismay at the sight of this uninviting domicile, she laconically observed there was that or none, unless I chose to sleep in a four-bedded room which

John Chesley's Inn, built in the 1820s for this prominent hotelkeeper. Photo by Pat MacKenna.

had three tenants in it—and those gentlemen. This alternative I somewhat indignantly declined, and in no very good humour retired to my cabin, where vile familiars to the dormitory kept us from closing our weary eyelids till the break of day (Guillet, Edwin C., *Pioneer Inns and Taverns*, Vols. III and IV, Toronto: Ontario Publ. Co. Ltd., 1958, p. 17.)

The Cline House (203 Second Street East) has been home to the Cornwall Public Library collection since 1955. A red brick building with a hipped roof covered with tin shingles, the Cline House was built in 1854 after the marriage of Samuel Cline and Margaret Dickinson.

Knox-St. Paul's United Church (108 Second Street East) was designed by the Toronto firm of Gordon and Helliwell and built in the Gothic style in 1885. Initially a Presbyterian Church, it sustained damage in the 1944 earthquake and has undergone alterations subsequently.

The First Baptist Church (130 Sydney Street) was built in 1884. The church gives evidence of the Gothic Revival style in the pointed arches of its windows. The house of worship for Baptists in Cornwall until 1960, the church now serves as a community hall.

St. John's Presbyterian Church (28 Second Street East) was erected in 1988-89. Dr. John Bethune was a moving force behind the construction of this church. This was the third home of the Presbyterian congregation in Cornwall. The original facade—once dominated by turrets and pinnacles—has been simplified over the years.

Cornwall Grammar School was built in 1806 to serve as John Strachan's woodframe grammar school. Strachan introduced formal education to Cornwall. A brick building was built in 1856 to serve boys and girls. The present building, which stands on the northeast corner of Sydney and Fourth Streets, replaced the second grammar school.

Rossi Artistic Glass (450 Seventh Street West) is the original Canadian manufacturer of artistic free form glass, and has been producing heritage cranberry glass for many years. From Monday to Friday Rossi offers free tours of its premises. The glass blowers are fascinating to watch as they shape a molten ball into a lovely form.

Pioneer Corner Craft Co-op is located by the side of Highway 2 west of the city center about 4 kilometers. Over 20 local craftspeople display and sell their work in two century-old log cabins. The quality of Stanley McNairn's honey and the excellence of the handicrafts make this a worthwhile stop.

The United Counties Museum (731 Second Street West) is located in the Wood house, built around 1840 by William Wood from limestone intended for a blockhouse which never materialized. Descendants of the family lived in the house until 1953, and in

One of two log buildings at the Pioneer Crafts Cooperative. Photo by Pat MacKenna.

1956 the Stormont, Dundas, and Glengarry Historical Society opened the United Counties Museum in the house. The Museum's collection traces local social and industrial history. It houses a vast collection of local memorabilia and Canadiana.

Le Village

Industrial development in Cornwall's east end flourished with the completion of the Cornwall Canal in 1843. In 1846 the government granted waterpower privileges to operate various mills, and within twenty years a grist and saw mill, a pottery, distillery, foundry, and woolen mill had been built on land adjacent to the east end of the canal. When a fire destroyed the woolen mill in 1870, town councilors offered the Montreal owners a bonus to rebuild. Dundas Mill was completed by 1872 and its success led to the construction of Canada Cotton Mill.

Many French Canadians came to Cornwall to work in the mills. The east end of Cornwall retains evidence of its French Canadian heritage, and the French sector is still referred to as "Le Village."

The Church of the Nativity of the Blessed Virgin (300 Montreal Road) was built between 1887 and 1892. Designated an historic building, the interior was renovated as a Centennial project and it was elevated to Co-Cathedral status in 1976. It incorporates features of Gothic design, buttressed walls, pointed arches, and vertical proportions. There is a Provincial plaque on the grounds proclaiming the French presence in

Former curator Alda MacKinnon in front of
the United Counties Museum, 1967.
Photo by Ken Gosling, courtesy the S. D. & G.
Historical Society.

Cornwall. The Church steeple is highly visible all through Le Village.

Continue west on Montreal Road to Baldwin Street where Nativity School is located. This was Cornwall's first French School. It was constructed in 1886 at the corner of Montreal Road and Edward Street. A second girls' school was added in 1924 and a separate boys' school opened in 1928. Now part of a larger school complex behind Nativity Church at 146 Chevrier Avenue, the boy's school is still standing and is one example of Cornwall's fine early 20th century brick structures.

Dundas Mill, located on Harbour Road, was built in 1870 by the Cornwall Manufacturing Company. A good example of late 19th century industrial architecture, its most dramatic feature was a multi-storey bell tower. Dundas Mill integrated with Canada and Stormont Mills in 1870 to form the Canadian Coloured Cottons Company. The existing building gives an indication of the size and character of a large industrial complex of the last century.

The Canada Mill, embellished with an Italianate facade, is just east of the base of McConnell Avenue South. Built in 1872, a decade later the world's largest weave shed was added. Employing 1,500 hands, this was the first factory in Ontario to use electric lighting which was installed under the supervision of Thomas Edison. The mill's looms and spindles were powered by a water turbine and two Corliss steam engines. By 1882 a dye house, gasworks, warehouses, workers' residences, and a weave shed were integrated into the plant. The mill ceased operation in 1959.

To the east of Marina 200, a short walk will take you to Cornwall's harbor where the replica steamship Canadian Empress of the Canadian Cruise Line makes regular stops during the summer and fall. From here you can see the remains of the Dundas and Canada mills built in the 1880s. William Mattice, son of a Loyalist, arranged the construction of a power canal, and laid out the east end industrial park in the 1860s. The uniquely shaped Mattice Park (also known as Dollard Park) is in the area of Edward and Lennox Streets. Close to the harbor is a foundry where J. Loney produced ploughs, boilers, and engines in the 1870s. W. Deruchie took over in 1886 and sold the foundry to W. Bingley in 1922. The doors were closed recently due to the changing economic climate.

St. Lawrence College of Applied Arts & Technology now occupies land that used to be St. Lawrence Park on Windmill Point, a popular picnic and swimming spot.

Courtauld's (1150 Montreal Road), Canada's first artificial silk or rayon plant, opened in 1924 just across from St. Lawrence Park. The plant is still in operation today producing viscose. This was the last stop to the east on the street car line. The trams made the return journey when the driver reversed the trolley line, flipped the seat backs the other way, and carried the fare box to the driving controls at the other end.

Finally, at 3332 Montreal Road, just before the Boundary Road exit to Highway 401, there is the restored 14 room cottage built in 1816. Once occupied by Nor'Westers John McDonald of Garth and John Duncan Campbell, it is now the Inverarden Regency Cottage Museum, covered in detail in Chapter 1, The Perch Route.

Festivals

Cornwall's yearly Canada Day weekend multi-cultural festival provides a wonderful opportunity to sample foods native to other countries and enjoy ethnic singing and dancing. Worldfest/ Festimonde is another celebration that brings visitors from all nationalities to the city for a week of dancing and parades on Pitt Street, and features daily performances at the Civic complex. The sound of bagpipes honors St. Andrew's Day and Robert Burn's birthday when there is dancing to music by fiddlers from Glengarry County and Cornwall's own Scottish band The Brigadoons. Traditional highland dancing is alive and well in the area.

Le Village is a good place to eat, drink, and be merry during the annual La Semaine Française/ French Week celebrations in June. Of course it's an interesting place to explore on foot at any time.

Accommodations

Johnson's Bed & Breakfast offers three large comfortable guest rooms. A home cooked breakfast is served in the dining room or on the sundeck. Contact: Michelyne & Edward Johnson, 1002 Pescod Avenue, Cornwall, Ontario, K6J 2J9, (613) 933-0398.

Gravelle's Bed & Breakfast features attractively furnished guest rooms, living room, and sun deck. Home cooked breakfast in dining room. Contact Betty & Bernard Gravelle, 1514 Francis Anne Avenue, Cornwall, Ontario K6H 2L2, (613) 938-0227.

Directions

A good night's rest and a fortifying breakfast should prepare you for our next tour which begins in Iroquois, west of Cornwall on Highway 401. This is the starting point for the Loyalist Front Route.

CHAPTER 5

The Loyalist Front Route

Preamble

Before the waters of Lake St. Lawrence flooded the old Loyalist Front along the St. Lawrence River, this area was world famous for the Long Sault Rapids and tourism. While the coming of the St. Lawrence Seaway and Hydro Power Project altered the landscape forever, it has not diminished the region's tourist potential or historical wealth, as revealed in this tour by Rosemary (Empey) Rutley, a fifth generation Canadian of German-Dutch (Palatinate) Loyalist origin. Striving to keep the secrets and folklore drowned by the waters of the Seaway alive, Rosemary takes us from the locks at Iroquois to Morrisburg along old Highway No. 2, then on to Prehistoric World, the battlefield of Crysler's Farm, Upper Canada Village, and finally to the Upper Canada Bird Sanctuary.

I.B.

History

"The Front," as it was known in the pre-St. Lawrence Seaway days, has a history rich and lively. The colonists, mostly United Empire Loyalists, settled along the shores of the St. Lawrence River, their only connection with downstream Montreal and Quebec. These pioneers worked hard and hewed a life for themselves from the forests that bordered the banks of the huge river, and the generations since have never forgotten their humble beginnings.

West of Cornwall the settlements began to coalesce with the completion of the Williamsburg Canals dug to circumvent the rapids across from Farran's Point, Morrisburg, and Iroquois in 1847. Once operational, the canals turned the villages of Mille Roches, Moulinette, Dickinson's Landing, Farran's Point, Morrisburg, and Iroquois into river ports and mill towns.

Since the arrival of the Loyalists, the Front has been a magnet to visitors, who have commented upon the mighty and untamed St. Lawrence River. In 1843 a British officer on board the propeller ship *Meteor* wrote of his trip from Iroquois to Cornwall:

> Leaving Prescott . . . we are now prepared and put everything in order for the descent of the rapids, these first, the "Galopes" are only a slight indication of what is to follow, but here is first exemplified the peculiar form of the bed of the river which marks most of the rapids in the St. Lawrence.

THE LOYALIST FRONT ROUTE

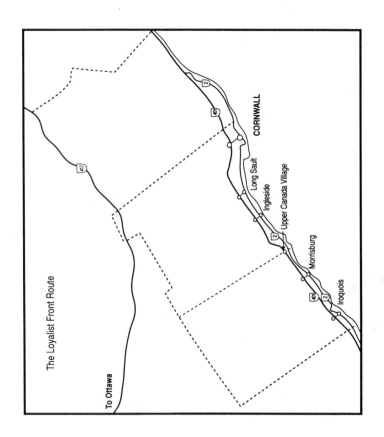

The Chutes are formed by walls or dykes of rock crossing the bed of the river with gaps in them through which the channels pass down to the head of these chutes [where] there is generally deep water from the fact that all the softer materials have been worn away by the violence of the stream and deposited in a shoal . . . below. The shallows in other parts consist of boulders of hard pan and blue clay . . . Emerging from the narrow channel between the islands, the whole rapids burst upon our view; for a minute I held my breath, as the enormous cellar right in front seemed ready to swallow us up, but the head of the boat was gradually turned to the south and at railroad speed we swept onward past the chute, only regretting that the rapid water did not continue longer. "Up sail, and fire up" was now the order, on we dashed in fine style. What a beautiful part of the country is this! Green meadows sloping to the waters edge, thick wooded islands, foaming rapids and calm quiet bays, busy life too in its happiest mood, harvesting abundant crops, the golden wheat, the green and still flourishing Indian corn gave promise of comfort and happiness for the coming winter . . . Onward still we pass mills and villages on either hand, all redolent of life and wealth. Next is the rapid "Flat" a long flat rapid . . . Further on to the left is the battlefield of Chrysler's Farm, a name dear to Canadians and doubly from it being sufficiently remote to be allayed by feelings of regret for the brave fellows who fell there. We are approaching the famed "Long Sault" but our steamer took the south channel, thereby avoiding the splendid rapid of the north channel. The River on the south or American side, is confined between the high and gravely banks, clothed with dark hemlocks and mountain pines, giving some of the passes an alpine appearance, with a dark rapid current running form one point to another, through windings requiring considerable skill to avoid the rocks at the points, and the eddies and whirlpools of the bays; (once) the mill at the foot of the Island is passed . . . the whole splendour of the magnificent Long Sault rapid of the north shore bursts at once in view. This is one of nature's grandest efforts, and she is no niggard of them on the mighty St. Lawrence a great river. Leaping down a descent of fifty feet, vast masses of water confined by shoals and dykes of rock are thrown into the air from deep and boiling "chutes" and again whirled into eddies with a noise like the roar of thunder . . . A low rocky shoal in the middle of the river called "Crab Island" very dangerous to barges and rafts is then passed. Not far from this is Cornwall (*Roebuck Papers*, National Archives, MG24A1 9 Vol. 5).

Since the flooding of these great rapids by the Seaway dams, no such "white water" thrills remain

The Iroquois Power House, 1955. This and the Mille Roches Power House were the first two erected along the St. Lawrence River in 1901. Photo courtesy the S.D. & G. Historical Society, Inverarden Museum.

for travelers along The Front. But much of the history alluded to in this passage has been preserved for modern day travelers.

Directions

To begin our tour of the Loyalist Front, take Highway 401 to Iroquois. Take exit 738 south to this historic town.

Iroquois

Located near the southwestern extremity of Dundas County, Iroquois was settled by Loyalists in 1786. Growth was rapid after the opening of the canal, and in 1857 the village was incorporated.

Initially known as Cathcart, in honor of Lord Cathcart who had commanded British forces in Canada, on incorporation the town was renamed Iroquois after the tribe of Native Americans who originally inhabited the region. Iroquois Point was once their campground, a way-station on their way north in summer and south in winter.

The canal provided water power necessary to operate a flour and grist mill, and the village rapidly became a flour shipping port. During the 1880s Beach's roller mills, several sawmills, and a carriage factory all located in Iroquois, resulting in a period of steady growth.

The village's prosperity was guaranteed by the arrival of Caldwell Linens before World War I. Growing rapidly, Caldwell's became the economic mainstay of the community. Threatened by the flood of cheap imports during the 1950s, the firm was acquired by Dominion Textiles. Dominion has remained in Iroquois, and their Caldwell plant is the community's most important employer.

While the building of the Seaway undoubtedly altered the face of the town, Iroquois is unique among the so-called "lost villages" because it has retained its sense of community, even if subsequent growth has not been as dramatic as predicted.

In 1954 work began on the St. Lawrence Seaway and Power Project. This massive undertaking changed the character of the Front irrevocably. The entire town of Iroquois had to be moved. Aware of the town's distinct heritage, the Ontario Hydro Electric Power Commission faced the unpleasant task of telling the residents that not only were they to give up their land, but that it was to vanish forever under a lake.

During the construction of the St. Lawrence Seaway, Ontario Hydro relocated the entire village by moving it approximately one kilometer north, transporting more than 150 houses on gigantic housemovers, and buying the other houses on generous terms to ease the purchase of new ones. This large scale move involved 280 homes and 1,110 people, in addition to commercial properties, schools, churches, and municipal offices. Because the village was so close to the mid-river International Boundary, it was chosen as the Canadian terminus of the International dam built to control water levels of the

Seaway. A canal was cut leaving Iroquois Point an island.

The choice of replacement lots was a delicate problem. Owning a premium lot in old Iroquois entitled one to a premium lot in New Iroquois. A river lot owner received a river lot. A secondary lot owner who wanted a premium lot in the new town paid the difference and a premium owner who wanted a secondary lot received a bonus. When a satisfactory agreement could not be reached, the courts decided the amount.

In Iroquois 30 to 40 landowners were expropriated. These people farmed at Iroquois Point. One farmer contested the offer he received because he owned a valuable orchard with trees in varying stages of development, and his demands were so high that the case had to go to the Exchequer Court. A separate valuation was made for each tree—and there were thousands of trees—before all parties were satisfied.

The Canal Coordinator for the St. Lawrence Seaway Authority lives in the yellow house on the hill by the Iroquois Locks—the only house left on the Point. The Tindale family originally lived here and the road beside the house led straight through their large orchard. Ontario Hydro has maintained the house well and has not altered the architecture. A family name scratched on a wall years ago can still be seen on one piece of woodwork.

One day I visited the Iroquois Locks when the lockmaster and the linesmen were passing an ocean vessel through the gates. The lockmaster's position is an enviable one that must be earned by starting at the bottom and working up. There are no lockmistresses at present, but there is one lineswoman who works in the maintenance department, and there are two lineswomen who come in for the summer.

Ships from all over the world use the Iroquois Locks. During the summer some 2,000 pleasure boats pass through, along with many smaller ones that make use of two little openings in the dam intended for that purpose. Ships may pass day or night unless storms occur, in which case the craft will anchor or tie to a wall until the weather clears and passage resumes. Language usually poses no problem as all pilots of foreign ships must be able to communicate in English. The day of my visit, traffic control, which gives positions of ships within the system coming from Lake Ontario at different times of the day, had reported that five ships were on their way. Ships come east from the Great Lakes—their last stop traveling from Toronto or Hamilton to Montreal or Quebec City where they might finish off a load of cargo before heading for the open sea. Westbound ships are headed for the Great Lakes.

The Seaway is now an integral part of Canada's economy. In 1978—a peak year—60 million tons of cargo passed through the locks. An average year may see 5 million tons of grain processed by the Seaway Authority.

Iroquois, however, has a long history as a transhipment point for various kinds of cargo. During Prohibition, for instance, it played a central role, as the following story illustrates.

The Carman House, near Iroquois, built between 1809 and 1825, is a typical Georgian farmhouse. Photo by Ian Bowering.

Story

Local raconteur and fox hunter Frank Sisty remembers when three local men went down the hill one night to a blind pig to have a drink. One of the men was wearing a black cap which resembled that of a policeman. As the two men neared the door they met a man running toward them looking incredibly upset.

"Officer," he pleaded, "I'll give you $25 if you don't mention my name and I'll go straight home!" The three rascals went inside and drank all night on the $25.

Visitors to Iroquois should walk or drive about the town at a leisurely pace to capture its true aura. Carman Road runs south toward the river, past Thompson Lumber and the feed store, to the Iroquois Lawn Bowling Club. Jimmy Everetts originally owned the old farm that the Lawn Bowling Club has turned into their club house.

Carman House Museum is located farther down the street on the left side. The museum offers crafts and samples of the past. The son of Michael Carman Jr. built this house on land granted to him as the son of a Loyalist. He and his wife farmed the 200 acres overlooking the St. Lawrence River until they could afford to build a larger house for their family of seven sons and two daughters. One can picture the pioneers performing their daily chores at this beautiful little farmhouse. A typical Georgian structure, the Carman House was constructed between 1809 and 1825 by Michael Carman on the family's original Loyalist land grant.

The home was preserved by the village as a Museum to commemorate the Centennial of Confederation in 1967.

Around the corner and down to the left stands a row of boathouses, the site of the original locks. Toward the west lies old Highway 2 and although it is now no more than a path, it leads straight into Cardinal, another riverside town. Once, when Ambert Brown's family was young, there was delay at the bridge over the canal in Cardinal, so he drove his car down this old road to get home faster. His wife was not impressed. Like Frank Sisty, Ambert Brown is a fine local storyteller. He arrived in Iroquois in 1935 looking for a job and remembers the old town:

> I was impressed with Iroquois from day one as it was quite different, sandwiched between the railroad on one side with the old steam engines snorting and puffing day and night and the most beautiful river, the mighty St. Lawrence on the other, its lake boats moving in and out of the locks with black smoke clouds curling to the sky. The smell of the burning coal was ever present in the village.

Ambert liked the place so much he married a local girl, Nelda Fader, and raised a family. Both Ambert and Frank have been recognized as local "treasures," each having won the Citizen of the Year Award. As "good old boys" from a past era, they remember Davis' Gas Station, Hess' Barber Shop and Louie the hickory nut vendor.

The road west by Carman House leads to the locks and a picnic area with benches for watching passing ocean liners. The Pioneer Cemetery near the locks offers the history buff a pleasurable wander among the old gravestones. One of the earliest markers is the tombstone of a Henry Brown who died in 1829, age 20 years. Another simple marble slab reads: "John De Groat, a soldier of 1784 Revolution, died June 23, 1852, age 87 years." A heart suspended on an iron frame marks the memorial to somebody's loved one and a huge field stone indicates the grave of another. An impressive monument identifies the resting places of the Beaches and Mulloys who were well known Iroquois families. Six generations of one family are buried in this cemetery.

The face in one of the trees in front of the graveyard fascinates many who believe in the supernatural. It apparently appeared after the Seaway was built and no one knows why. Perhaps it's a lost soul from pre-Seaway times, or an irate citizen denied a resting spot within the gates. Some say it's the face of a Native who once lived here.

At the east side of town some old houses remain—old family homes of the Millers, Dillaboughs, and Fergusons. The Anglican cemetery down the road has been elevated and preserved—a wonderful old graveyard.

The Martins' old stone home, 52 Elizabeth Street, nestles among the new and updated houses and is one of the town's historical landmarks. Other streets boast more grand old buildings hobnobbing with the sleek, modern ones.

Visitors to the area might be interested to know that more than a kilometer west of Iroquois, on Highway 2, stands the stone residence of a man who owned extensive tracts of land in Matilda Township, Allan MacDonell. Simon Fraser, who discovered the Fraser River in British Columbia, married Allan's daughter Catherine, and they are both buried in the historic cemetery at St. Andrew's north of Cornwall. Many other old stone houses line the highway west of Iroquois, and many travelers find it worthwhile taking a drive west to Cardinal to see them, and to view the old canal ruins that run through the village.

Morrisburg

Our next stop is east of Iroquois, however, on Highway 2. Upon entering Morrisburg from Iroquois on Highway 2 visitors should turn south at the lights and proceed in that direction toward the waterfront. A boat launch, a beach, and a park complete with barbecues ensures great outdoor recreation. Lakeshore Drive and First Street— which is one street north—both offer superb examples of century-old architecture. You'll find elegant brick homes and some churches with magnificent stained glass windows.

An interesting alternative route takes you along Lakeshore Drive east of Iroquois to Mariatown, which was one of the first places settled by the Loyalists. There are some wonderful old homes, and the scenery is lovely. Highway 2 will bring you right into Morrisburg, to the riverside park and the boat launch.

Like Iroquois, Morrisburg, or "West Williamsburg," as it was called before it became a village in the 1860s, was another staunch riverside neighborhood. Unlike Iroquois, it was only partially flooded by the Seaway. Originally a farming community, its farms faced the St. Lawrence and ran in narrow spans back from the river. It was named after James Morris from Brockville, the first Postmaster-General of Canada, who was noted for *reducing* postage from 16¢ to 5¢.

The first settlers in the area were German or Palatine United Empire Loyalists who came with their families from the Mohawk River Valley to Canada, walking through dense forests late in the fall of 1783, leaving everything behind to face a cold winter and a future of poverty and hardship. They traveled up the Richelieu River, over Lake Champlain to Sorel, and up the St. Lawrence to Montreal and Cornwall. To determine the location of their respective properties, the men drew lots from a hat. Each was entitled to 100 acres on the river front and two hundred acres back. A married man received fifty more acres for his wife and fifty for each child—who would also receive two hundred additional acres upon coming of age or at marriage.

These Loyalists arrived in the spring of 1784 and worked cutting timber for the Montreal market. Many soon found the large parcels of land too much to handle and sold their children's grants to immigrants. Before the canal was built some colonists became teamsters towing boats upriver or carrying passengers and goods between Cornwall and Prescott. Only after the canal was finished in the 1840s and steam tugs appeared did they settle down to farm their land.

Story

Who are the Palatine Loyalists? The Palatinate is an area situated on the south bank of the Rhine River, immediately north of Alsace-Lorraine. During the religious and national wars waged in 17th century Europe, Louis XIV of France invaded the Palatinate, exiling its Protestant inhabitants in the wake of his victory. Looking for new homes and a sympathetic political climate as many as 15,000 immigrated to England by 1709. As chance would have it a group of Mohawk Chiefs from the Colony of New York were touring London. Seeing the plight of these refugees, the Chiefs invited the Palatines to settle in the Mohawk Valley, along the Schohaire River.

Taking up this offer, 3,200 Palatines set out for the 13 Colonies in 1710. They remained loyal to George III throughout the American Revolution. Many of them served with Sir John Johnson's King's Royal Regiment of New York and followed Johnson north after the War to settle in present day Osnabruck, Williamsburg, and Matilda Townships in the Counties of Stormont and Dundas.

In the 1800s Morrisburg boasted McKenzie's Saw Mill, Nash's Machine Shop, Austin Doran's Carding

Mill, and the lockmaster's house. A stagecoach road trailed along the river bank past wharves loaded with goods on the way to the United States. The arrival of the Grand Trunk Railway brought business—stores, churches, a hotel, a bakery, and a thriving sash and door factory. The British financed the construction of the railway because the few wealthy people in Canada at that time felt it was a poor risk. Farmers, too, were skeptical because they feared harm might be done to their cattle and themselves if a railway were to cross their lands. However, an agreement was reached and about 1,700 tradesmen, 4,000 laborers, and 1,000 horses worked on the project. The road bed and track were among the best on the continent, and the first train began its trip between Montreal and Brockville on 17 September 1855. The railway ensured Morrisburg's growth and prosperity for many years, as Morrisburg native Eleanor Wickware Morgan wrote in her book, *Up the Front: A Story of Morrisburg*:

> The old town hall on the corner of East Main Street and Isabella St. was the market place of these days and after the railway came, on market days the road from the corner of the Gravel road (Highway 31 now) and Main Street was one continuous line of lumber wagons, loaded with produce. Morrisburg in those days was the center of trade for the whole country. On one occasion a farmer from Finch sold a single load of butter for $402.

THE LOYALIST FRONT ROUTE

Grand Trunk Railway locomotive 1008. Both the engine and the Aultsville Station were moved to Crysler Park, just west of Upper Canada Village as a permanent memorial to the Milkrun Moccasin train that had run between Brockville and Montreal, return daily, from 1855 to 9 August 1958. Photo courtesy of the S. D. & G. Historical Society, Inverarden Museum.

Because of financial problems the railway was taken over by the Federal Government in 1920 and has been operated by Canadian National Railways since 1923. In 1957 Aultsville Station and Grand Trunk Railway locomotive 1008 were moved to Crysler Park, just west of Upper Canada Village as a permanent memorial to the Railway that had served the waterfront communities since 1855. The *Moccasin* train that had made a daily return trip from Brockville to Montreal last ran on 9 August 1958.

In Morrisburg's main street, blocks were built either by or for local prominent families: Bradfield, Tait, Beckstead, Farlinger, Hesson, and McDonald. There was a music hall built in 1879 by the Merkleys located in the Merkley Block. This hall became the center of Morrisburg's culture and entertainment. In those days you could watch horse races on the canal, go on snowshoe parties, and if you were a youngster you would probably hitch rides on the bobsleds that hauled wood, hay, and blocks of ice into town. You would surely take in the annual Sunday School picnic on Corrigan's Island, and the Agricultural Fair each September—sneaking into the sideshow to watch the Wild Man from Borneo, the Fat Man, and the Sword Swallower. The lovelorn of the village could find their match at the matrimonial bureau of Miss Sara Lambert from New York who guaranteed her clients a speedy and happy marriage.

Morrisburg's entire business section was flooded by the St. Lawrence Seaway and Power project in the 1950s. Much of the residential area was relocated to the east of the original village, and the old locks disappeared completely.

Riverside Heights

Located a few kilometers east of Morrisburg on the north side of Highway 2, Riverside Heights is our next stop.

The Whitney Memorial (Holy Trinity) Church was built in Morrisburg in 1903 and was moved to Riverside Heights in 1957 during the construction of the St. Lawrence Seaway. In the graveyard behind the church one can view the headstones of Sir James Pliny Whitney and his family. Conservative Premier of Ontario from Williamsburg Township, Whitney served from 1905 until his death in 1914. He was born a blacksmith's son on October 2, 1853 and became a lieutenant in the militia during the Fenian raids of 1866. In 1876 he opened a law office in Morrisburg, and in 1896 he was elected opposition Leader of the Conservative Party. When the Conservatives swept the province in 1905 James Whitney became Ontario's premier. He was knighted in 1908.

Perhaps one the most skilled propagandists in Ontario's history, Whitney's famous epitaph, "Bold enough to be honest, and honest enough to be bold," was coined by Whitney during a campaign speech attacking Liberal corruption. Whitney, a typical Edwardian politician, opposed women's right to vote.

Monument to Sir James Pliny Whitney, at Queen's Park, Toronto. Photo by Ian Bowering.

Prehistoric World

Further along Highway 2, north on Upper Canada Village Road, you will encounter Prehistoric World. This continuing project, started in 1981, is the result of a childhood dream for sculptors Paul Dupuis and his brother Serge. They consider it a commendable way to be financially independent without having to part with their artistic work. Several years ago they came from northern Ontario in search of the ideal place "that felt right," found it, and began creating full-size prehistoric animals that capture the visitors' imaginations as well as their hearts.

Like most newborn projects, the first years of operation were tough. Now the main problem for Paul and Serge is finding time to work on their models because they insist on doing all the labor themselves.

Prehistoric World nestles in the forest, its antediluvian dwellers waiting among the trees. The exhibit is one of the biggest in the world. One brontosaurus weighs in at 40 tons and took 1000 hours to complete. It's a simple concept—a botanical garden in someone's back yard, 153 acres of 40 full-sized dinosaurs made of reinforced concrete for children to touch and see. Adults may appreciate the dinosaurs at a different level and enjoy the literature available on these ancient creatures. Visitors may follow nature trails through the forest where giant creatures from the past appear suddenly in front of them at almost every corner, peering down through the leaves of the trees. The same people

Prehistoric World sculptor Paul Dupuis with
one of his latest creations, a Parasaurolophus.
Photo by Rosemary Rutley.

come back each year, says Paul, to see what's been added. The Dupuis brothers try to create something different each season. Their unique idea is paying off, and they are fulfilling a childhood dream as well as enhancing the community's culture.

Prehistoric World is not designed for all day entertainment. The park is not a playground, and children must be accompanied by an adult. Most visitors appreciate the delightful scenery and exhibits for an hour or two and then go to a nearby restaurant for lunch, or to Crysler Beach for a picnic.

At the end of the summer season the park remains open weekends until mid-October. Autumn is a great time to visit, as there are fewer tourists and, of course, fewer mosquitoes.

Monument to the Battle of Crysler's Farm, War of 1812

This monument is located 11 kilometers east of Morrisburg on the grounds of Upper Canada Village. The monument commemorates the Battle of Crysler's Farm, which was fought on 11 November 1813. It sits on a hill near the site of John Crysler's farmland, now submerged by the Seaway, overlooking the broad expanse of the St. Lawrence River.

Standing on the hill by the monument, one can picture a flotilla of American soldiers creeping covertly downstream on its way to attack Montreal, and a group of farmers banding together in the nearby field to protect their homesteads against fierce American assault, or maybe some members of the

Canadian militia preparing to defend their newfound freedom.

At the decisive Battle of Crysler's Farm 800 Canadian and British soldiers defeated 1,800 Americans. The war itself was caused by conflicts over Maritime rights between Great Britain and the United States. The latter was no match for Britain on the seas, but planned to proceed down the St. Lawrence and capture Montreal thus striking Great Britain at her most vulnerable point. Although superior in numbers, artillery, and cavalry, the American forces met with such withering fire that they fled from the battlefield, and Montreal was temporarily safe. After many skirmishes both sides knew that a victory would be costly, so on Christmas Eve 1814 they signed the Treaty of Ghent to end the war.

Upper Canada Village

The Ontario government created Upper Canada Village to preserve some of the local historic buildings that would otherwise have been destroyed during the construction of the Seaway in the 1950s. This pioneer village museum displays artifacts from the time of Confederation, while costumed characters move about the village recreating life as it was in pioneer days.

A cardboard replica of a smiling woman in pioneer dress proudly sporting the sash of The Total Abstinence Society greets the visitors at Upper Canada Village. They might even encounter her in person preaching the evils of drink to guests at

Willard's Hotel. This smiling matron is Flora MacPherson, the temperance lady. Many tourists have been known to drone "Throw Down the Bottle" with Flora while they sign the abstinence pledge and pose for snapshots.

Flora MacPherson is really Jean Jeacle, the Interpretive Entertainment Officer for Upper Canada Village. Jean, a local playwright and teacher, is initiating a first person program in which village characters come alive through role-play and communicate with visitors on that level.

Jean began as the teacher in the village schoolhouse. Like the other interpreters she informed visitors about life in 1860s. Jean soon discovered that her audience found the experience more meaningful when she impersonated the character instead of merely reciting historical facts. Soon Jean left the school house and created her character, Myrtle Mumphries and her "Merry Minstrels." This troupe performed in a tent, singing songs, and enacting melodramas of the 1860s. Racy Myrtle met with such success that Jean invented Flora MacPherson, a staunch Methodist who goes about the town rallying for total abstinence. Flora knows the comings and goings of all the villagers, and offers her advice and opinions freely.

Although Flora is a fabrication, Jean has created a history for her character that might easily have been true. Flora was born in 1815 at the time of the Battle of Waterloo. Her father was wounded in the war and later turned to drink—here we find the root of Flora's activism. Her mother taught her to speak French, and to read, which explains Flora's

Jean Jeacle and Flora pose together at
Upper Canada Village. Photo by Rosemary Rutley.

education when most women of the day were illiterate. The death of her mother left Flora to care for two sisters and an older brother. In 1832 the family came to Canada where her father later died leaving Flora free at last. But how does an intelligent woman like Flora vent her energies in the 1860s? She spends time with the Sunday School and The Total Abstinence Society.

It takes a special kind of person to portray a character like this, says Jean. In addition to being a good actor you must be a good *re*actor, prepared for what someone might say back to you, and above all, she says, you must know the background information thoroughly. For example, Flora might not be expected to know much about the Reciprocity Treaty, but if she is asked what she had for breakfast or what she wears under her pioneer skirt she had better know.

The newspaper editor, the Lutheran pastor, and the tavern keeper now participate in the first person program, and visitors may come up and talk to them in that capacity. Small scenarios occur periodically throughout the day during which the characters do not interact with the audience the way the first person characters do, but through their dialogue they offer information about pioneer times. For instance, the new railway has brought better communications to the village; the mail arrives every day, and young men are now able to look farther afield for work. So one of the village women goes to the store hoping to get a letter telling her that her married daughter in Kingston has had her new baby. As soon as the mother hears that her grandchild is born, she will take the train to Kingston to be with her daughter, a trip that used to take four days. The woman strongly objects to a man—the doctor—tending her daughter instead of the customary midwife. All this she discusses with the storekeeper.

Although the village promises nothing specific at any given hour, visitors may be sure that something is happening somewhere all the time. As they wait for lunch on the porch of Willard's Hotel, perhaps Cyril Sweeney, another delightful village character, will sing some of his secular songs of which Flora so strongly disapproves. Maybe Flora herself will present her temperance demonstration. During July and August Flora encourages visitors to attend Sunday School classes or sing along at choir practice. The new Lutheran pastor has just arrived from America, and Flora believes that a young man in the pastor's position should have a wife, so there will be plenty of scope for new and exciting ideas to develop in the coming seasons.

The Village offers a complete vacation package which includes overnight accommodation in the area, an 1860s meal at Willard's Hotel, and perhaps a murder mystery to solve. This provides an excellent chance to see the Village by candlelight.

Several events that don't occur on a daily basis but do happen at special times of the year provide experiences just as they might have happened a century ago. Victoria Day celebrations are held in May, and Flora will be there with her pledge cards, as she believes that liquor and leisure go hand in hand. The sheep shearing weekend occurs in June, followed by the Communities Day in August. During both July and August Flora will guide you on lantern walks through the village.

Sometime in August, much to Flora's mortification, the risqué Mrs. Mumphries comes through with her Merry Minstrels. Mid-September brings the Fall Fair around the same time as the annual Art Show and Sale. Harvesting weekend in October winds up the summer season.

Upper Canada Village is open year-round. The off-season program varies each year. It offers heritage workshops, evening sleigh rides, and skating on the Village canal. There are weekend specials and guided tours through the village. Guests can enjoy dinner theater shows and leisurely walks during the changing seasons of fall, winter, and spring. The Village Store is open daily. Bring your family or book a group. Flora will be expecting you.

Upper Canada Migratory Bird Sanctuary

This sanctuary is located about 5 kilometers east of Upper Canada Village on the north shore of the St. Lawrence River.

He moves through the foraging flock raising his august head above the others, aware of every intrusion. Within the gaggle he ranks highly, pecking at other geese, who immediately scuttle out of his path. If it weren't for his snow-white feathers, one would think he was a Canada Goose like the other magnificent birds that call the St. Lawrence Parkway their summer home. But old Roy is a pilgrim gander, a domestic bird who longed for life in the fast lane and went for it. He's the namesake of a man called Roy

Barkley who drove the horses and stagecoach at Upper Canada Village for many years. One spring several years ago Roy acquired the young gander from a local farmer and brought him to the Village barnyard. That summer when a low-flying flock of Canada Geese honked over head, the stouthearted young bird uttered a few squawks and took off to join them. Later that year he was spotted with the flock near the Upper Canada Migratory Bird Sanctuary east of Upper Canada Village. Workers at the Sanctuary named him after the stagecoach driver, and since then the dauntless bird has achieved the impossible dream. Old Roy and his mate, a Canada Goose, nest on a small island near the Sanctuary. Their sterile eggs are replaced each year with fertile ones from another Canada Goose. The audacious old fellow migrates with the flock each year and has so endeared himself to the employees that former worker Bryce Rupert, who has followed the bird's activities over the years, sports a set of license plates featuring the gander's name.

Upper Canada Bird Sanctuary has many things to offer the nature-loving traveler. Summer home to over 2,000 Canada Geese, the Sanctuary consists of wooded uplands, goose pastures, tilled fields, waterways, and marshland spread over 9,000 hectares of land. It opened in 1961 on lands acquired by the St. Lawrence Parks Commission after the construction of the St. Lawrence Seaway. The local flock was established by releasing 55 geese from Central Ontario in 1959, and 15 mated pairs of geese from south of the

A 1960 photograph of Al Raymond tagging a Canada Goose at the Upper Canada Migratory Bird Sanctuary. Photo courtesy of the S.D. & G. Historical Society, Inverarden Museum.

border in 1960. More than 4,000 birds have descended from these geese and from the goose flock of the New York State Wilson Hill Wildlife Management Area across the St. Lawrence.

The interpretive center near the banding pond explains the history and management activities of the Sanctuary, and the viewing tower nearby provides a place for watching the goose and duck activity in the pond, as well as deer grazing in the nearby fields. Visitors and many local people combine walking exercise with natural pleasure by taking advantage of the many nature trails at the Sanctuary. These trails are self-guided from mid-May to mid-October but walks are conducted twice daily in July and August.

More than 50 deer stay at the Sanctuary during the spring and summer, and twice as many during the winter. Visitors can see them in the fields along the entrance road at dawn and dusk but because the white-tails are particularly active during March, April, May, and November, sightseers must drive carefully in and around the Sanctuary.

Both Bryce Rupert and Roy the coach driver have retired, but Old Roy the gander is still around. He is a wary old bird, and one must tread softly to get a glimpse of him. However, in your search, if you should spy a blue Mazda truck with "Old Roy" on the plates you'll know that you're in the right place. Come visit the Sanctuary and bring your camera to capture memories of some of these events:

- During the fall hunting season sportsmen may participate in a controlled waterfowl hunt. Some restrictions apply in addition to regular hunting rules.

• Duck banding at the Sanctuary takes place in late August to mid-October. For more information on this event contact the Ministry of Natural Resources in Cornwall.

• A feeding program which runs from September 15 to November 15 daily at 2:30 p.m. provides ample goose viewing opportunities.

• The Sanctuary offers a series of Fresh Air Experiences to Elementary School Classes. These programs combine hikes, games, hands-on exercises, and group discussions which are aimed at helping students understand the environment and the part they play in it. For more information on this and the bird feeding operation contact the St. Lawrence Parks Commission in Morrisburg.

• Visitors may fish in Lake St. Lawrence adjacent to the Sanctuary either from the shore or by launching their boats at one of many of the launch sites on the lake.

Directions

To return to Cornwall (or Ottawa or Montreal), take Highway 401 east from Upper Canada Village. Our next tour takes us underwater to the sites and memories of the Lost Villages. There is much to see even if you can't scuba dive.

CHAPTER 6

The Lost Villages Adventure

40 Miles of Cool Water: The Seaway Song

Come down to Cornwall the Seaway Town
There is lots of activity going around
Where they're digging big ditches and
pulling up ground
Come on all you people to the Seaway Town.

(By permission of Mrs. L. Burgess, Cornwall, sung to a tune similar to "Betsy from Pyke.")

Preamble

During the 1950s and beyond, the flooding of the upper St. Lawrence Valley, west of Cornwall, to create the St. Lawrence Seaway and Hydro Power Project was viewed by many as progress. Seen in engineering terms—it was indeed a job well done. But what of the human cost?

Free-lance writer Glenda Eden, of German-Scottish descent, born after the flooding and raised in the new town of Ingleside, records some of this human story through the memories of such people as former Mille Roches Powerhouse operator Archie Eastman who will "always remember it the way it was." Glenda will also introduce you to Native-trained healer Granny Hoople, the pioneers' first 'doctor' who lived to age 91. And to view the villages drowned by Lake St. Lawrence, you will be taken on an underwater marine heritage tour by divers from Save Ontario Shipwrecks and feel "the current run through your hair instead of the wind" as you stand on the submerged superstructure of an old bridge. Glenda will return you to shore to tour Upper Canada Playhouse and Old Author's Farm, both in Morrisburg. By the time you are finished you will appreciate that here, as in the rest of Eastern Ontario, heritage is inextricably linked with the present. For many, the Lost Villages will not be forgotten.

I. B.

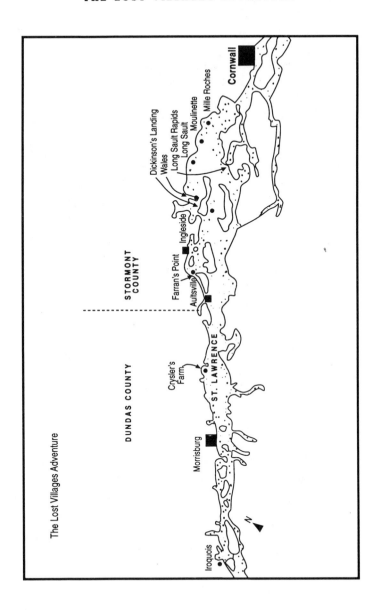

History

Surely one of the most fascinating chapters in Eastern Ontario's history is that of the Lost Villages.

On 10 August 1954 international sod turning ceremonies at Cornwall, Ontario, and Massena, New York, marked the official start of work on the 1,640,000 kilowatt St. Lawrence Seaway and Power Project, culminating over 135 years of work towards a navigable Canadian waterway to the Great Lakes, and more than 250 years of effort to connect the river to Quebec City.

Once the project was officially started, 50 years of uncertainty were over in Eastern Ontario. As historians Frances and Clive Martin wrote in their book *Stormont, Dundas and Glengarry: 1945-1978*, once the work was completed people hoped that "Progress could continue unimpeded; the region would grow rapidly and become wealthy."

Undertaken jointly by Ontario Hydro and the New York State Power Authority with the necessary enabling legislation from the United States Congress (Wiley-Dondero Act) and the Canadian Parliament, the construction of the Seaway has been called by some the first step towards 'Free Trade' and the eventual annexation of Canada to the United States. Politics aside, the construction of the Seaway and Power Project was a gigantic feat that many old-timers claim even changed the local weather.

In human terms it meant the removal of the old villages of Iroquois, Aultsville, Farran's Point, Dickinson's Landing, Wales, Moulinette, and Mille

Roches; the partial submersion of the town of Morrisburg; and the creation of the model towns of (new) Iroquois, Long Sault, and Ingleside. It led to the development of the dormitory suburb of Riverside Heights, historic Upper Canada Village, and the drowning of the Long Sault Rapids. All of this was necessary to clear the way for the flooding of the river, and to make way for the headpond for the proposed powerhouse. In total 531 homes were moved, and some 6,500 Canadians were affected over a 20,000 acre area.

At 8 a.m. on 1 July 1958, 30 tons of dynamite were touched off to blow up the last coffer-dam which set in motion the inundation of these communities and the creation of Lake St. Lawrence which extends 45 kilometers from the powerhouse just west of Cornwall to the Iroquois Dam. With the headpond holding approximately 23 billion cubic feet of water, the dam located at Cornwall was the world's first International Hydro Electric Power Dam. Spanning the St. Lawrence from Cornwall in Canada to Barnhart Island near Massena in the U.S., the powerhouse is made up of two identical components. The official opening of the Seaway in 1959 led many to look forward to years of continued growth.

World leaders joined some 1.5 million tourists to visit the construction sites, and between 1951 and 1958 the population of the City and Township of Cornwall grew by 21%, while Matilda Township in Dundas County grew by 27%. The same growth was felt across the border in New York State.

It's easy to forget the sense of optimism felt by the "I like Ike" decade, and the reverence people felt towards the supremacy and inevitability of technological change. Nothing better illustrates these attitudes than the point made by Carleton Mabee, author of *The Seaway Story*, who wrote, "It is ironic that while the Seaway agencies kept precise records of how much steel and concrete went into the Seaway, they did not keep precise records of the number of persons the Seaway forced out of the way." Neither could the pundits know that the Seaway would operate at a loss until 1980 when toll rates were increased, and that within a year of the Seaway opening, Cornwall and area would suffer a series of plant closures due to foreign competition and poor management that would lead the federal government to label the City "depressed."

The construction of the Seaway brought money and jobs and interesting, exciting new people to the area. It was a boom time with the promise of wealth and lasting prosperity—a promise that some believe has never been fully realized. For many of the 6,500 people who were relocated it was the worst of times as they watched their farms and villages disappear under the water.

For many people the Lost Villages will always be lost, for others they are just now being found; and for sport divers such as John Van Baal they are being rediscovered. And for some people, such as Archie Eastman who lived and worked along the river, the Lost Villages are still there in memory, as vivid and clear as they were forty years ago.

Improving and expanding the St. Lawrence Seaway system had been an ambitious dream since the shores of the St. Lawrence were first settled. Attempts to by-pass rapids and harness the power of the river began as early 1689. In 1895 the United States and Canada developed a joint committee to study the development of the river, and for more than sixty years both governments debated and pondered the possibility of such a feat. After so many years of speculation, the project proceeded amazingly quickly; within four years of the sod turning ceremony in 1954, the Lost Villages were covered with water, and power was being generated. One year after that the Seaway was officially opened and the big ships began to travel *over* the Lost Villages.

The Lost Villages are the villages that no longer exist, the villages whose names are slowly leaving the vocabulary of the local people. For this reason Morrisburg and Iroquois are generally not considered "lost," but it should be noted that almost all of Iroquois was relocated, as was a substantial portion of Morrisburg. The relocation of the people from the Lost Villages created whole new communities with histories that begin in the 1950s. The communities have taken on new character, and although some houses were moved and many streets and parks bear the names of the Lost Villages, there are few similarities between the original Lost Villages and their namesakes.

The grand brick homes of Aultsville and Farran's Point could not be moved, nor could the massive trees and carefully tended gardens in Wales. Waterfront villages with melodic and romantic names like Mille Roches, Moulinette, and Dickinson's Landing have been replaced by acres of parkland

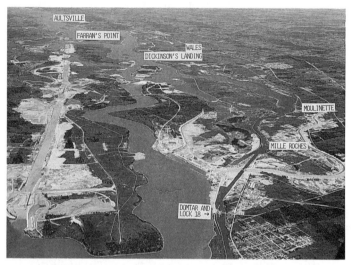

An aerial photo taken 15 June 1958 showing the Cornwall-Massena area before the flooding. Photo courtesy S.D. & G. Historical Society, Inverarden Museum.

operated by the St. Lawrence Parks Commission. In spite of the good intentions and genuine attempts by Ontario Hydro to treat people fairly and to preserve their homes, much was lost to the Seaway and Power project.

On "Inundation Day," thousands came to see the water rush over the villages. They came by car loads, some from great distances, to vie for the best vantage point. Many must have arrived before dawn for they were waiting at 8 a.m. on 1 July 1958 when the coffer dam blew. They came with lawn chairs, and coolers, and the odd case of beer to witness the inundation. It was to be a festive occasion, a highly publicized event complete with banners, souvenir wooden nickels, and commemorative silver spoons.

But not everyone was in a festive mood. Many of the locals who had been relocated to the new townsites of Ingleside and Long Sault were not enthusiastic. They'd had enough of the Seaway construction and the upheaval it had caused in their lives, and couldn't celebrate the flooding of their riverfront communities. Memories of that day are as varied as the people who were there.

Archie Eastman of Mille Roches went out to the site half-heartedly later in the day and remembers not only the general sense of remorse but the animals that scurried out of the water's path. Muskrats scrabbled and clung to anything solid, and in the next few days bags of frogs were taken away by those with a taste for them.

Eileen Merkley, also of Mille Roches, reluctantly followed some of her neighbors out to the site. She remembers people positioning their lawn chairs as close as possible to get a good view, and others, not trusting the engineers' guidelines, moving well back of the river, fearing they would be swept away by the water. Many were disappointed. The raging torrent of water that they expected would rush over the villages was only a trickle the first day, and would not completely cover the land for several more days. Even those with a more realistic understanding of the process were surprised at how long it actually took, Eileen says.

Fran Laflamme of Wales, who has become a Lost Villages expert of sorts, remembers Inundation Day with a certain amount of cynicism. She recalls that early that morning the heavens opened and a horrendous storm broke over the area. She says it was as if people were being reminded that there were still things bigger and more powerful than Ontario Hydro and what was about to happen. The hoopla that surrounded the blasting of the last coffer dam was almost entirely symbolic. "It's my understanding that it was actually the closing of the control dam gates near the power station that caused the flooding," Fran says. The water slowly crept over the banks of the river and by the fourth day hydro electric power was being generated.

The one sentiment they all express is the respect they acquired for the engineers involved. The proposed shoreline did not differ much from the actual shoreline that exists today.

There were those who'd had doubts. The bridge at the Long Sault entrance to the parkway was constructed well before the flooding began. Fran

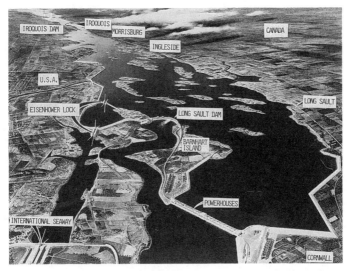

Artist's conception of the St. Lawrence Power Project as it would look after the flooding. Photo courtesy S. D. & G. Historical Society, Inverarden Museum.

Laflamme remembers tobogganing on the banks of Hoople Creek that last winter before the flooding and seeing this bridge. "It was stuck out there in the middle of a farmer's field and we thought 'How do they know where the water's going to go?' But they did. Go look at that bridge today. They weren't too far off."

Archie Eastman is an elderly man who at first introduction looks fit, and trim, and healthy but who has over the last few years been plagued with numerous ailments that required surgery. He tells of how, when he's fighting the effects of the anaesthetic, it's the river he hears roaring in his ears. He sees through the drugged haze the power of the Long Sault and the raging force of the river he grew up on. "Why do you think that is?" he asks, puzzled. But after you've listened to his stories and heard him tell of the life he lived on the river before the Seaway there seems to be no reason to ponder the question.

Archie grew up in old Mille Roches, what remained of the original town after the area was flooded near the turn of the century. The St. Lawrence Seaway and Power project of the 1950s was not the first attempt to alter the river to improve transportation and to harness its energy for electrical power. Canals were built along this stretch of the St. Lawrence in the mid-1800s and improved upon half a century later.

Archie was the chief operator at the Mille Roches Powerhouse, until it was closed down and the big generating station that we see on the river today began to produce hydro electric power. He spent his boyhood on the river and watched an amazing engineering feat unfold before him, saw rumor and speculation turn into reality.

"The Seaway for me and the wife started when we were maybe fifteen years old." He remembers the tripod-carrying surveyors wandering across his mother's yard when he was a teenager, telling them how the water was going to come right over their property. "How would you like to be able to fish right off your veranda?" a man said to us. "Cause this is where the water is going to be." Archie also remembers that the surveyors and engineers "just kept you more or less in the dark." The people along the St. Lawrence would continue to be kept in the dark for many years wondering what would become of their farms, houses, and businesses.

Across from Archie's home in old Mille Roches was Barnhart Island, a favorite haunt of his at a time when the border between Canada and the U.S. was more or less ignored by the people who lived on the river. It was the summer home of the wealthy Barnhart family and the year-round home of several farming families. Residents of this American island left years before Seaway construction began to be built. This busy little community included a cheese factory, a church, and graveyard, and was the site of early engineering tests. "They drilled so many holes it's a wonder it didn't sink," says Archie.

He remembers watching one of these families loading up and leaving their island home. He saw the weeping family cross the river by scow.

And then they started to drill out under the Sault. "Now the Long Sault Rapids," he says, "you'll never be able to understand what it was. It split storms, which is hard to believe unless you went up to the head of Barnhart Island and saw a storm coming." The energy of the rapids would split the sky.

"I fished out there in the moonlight, the week before they drained the rapids in April 1957, catching pickerel—Morris Fickes and I. And we'd get fifty to sixty of them pickerel, fishing there in the moonlight. And the next week you were walking on the bottom of that."

For many at the Front the draining of the rapids was the most important and moving event in the construction of the Seaway apart from the actual flooding of the villages. It was with a sense of awe and profound sadness that the people saw the mighty Sault finally tamed. It had drowned rivermen and taken their cargoes, but its power was respected and its beauty appreciated. Archie and others walked the drained rapid bed in disbelief, finding there the remains of rafts and other river craft that had not successfully navigated the course. They walked around the boulders carved into giant bowls by the eddies and whirlpools.

What Archie remembers is a way of life on the river that is no more, gone because of the Seaway, perhaps, but more likely gone because of the passing of the years. It was a time when your livelihood came from the river and the bounty of its shores. "My mother would say go down and get a pickerel for supper," Archie recalls. "We'd go down by this big stone and throw in our poles and we'd each have a couple of pickerel in 15 minutes. And fit to eat then! Beautiful."

And, as was common then all along the Front before the Seaway, they would also go over to the American side, to Barnhart Island to pick raspberries, strawberries, plums, and crabapples. "And nuts! There was no end of the butternuts we could pick," says Archie. "We lived off that. Nobody bothered us. We never saw a State Trooper."

This was a time our American neighbors were neighbors in the true rural sense of the word. They slipped back and forth across the river by scow to see the doctor, to shop, or to have their animal feed ground at the mill. Winter or summer, the St. Lawrence was a highway for the river people, isolated from each other only in the spring when it began to break up and the early winter before the water froze.

According to Archie, it didn't hold them up for very long. After a day or so of cold weather they'd brave their way across with a team of horses. He remembers vividly a trip across the river in early winter with a slightly built, white bearded farmer, two collie dogs, and a team. "We was going along and he started yelling at the horses and slapping them . . . we were no more off that ice and the river was open from shore to shore."

It was the habit of the river people to watch when the ice was treacherous and sound a horn if there was trouble. This proved to be an invaluable and welcome sound on one memorable trip Archie made across the river when the ice was starting to get soft. Young Archie, still in his early teens, was crossing from Barnhart Island with a farmer's horse and cutter. The farmer was watching to make sure the young lad made it across, and promptly sounded the horn when he saw the cutter slowly sink into the water near the shore at Mille Roches. The cutter had sunk, but the front legs of the horse remained on firm ice. "There wasn't much I could do," says Archie matter of factly, "but hold up the horse's head and wait for the horn."

The horn would summon a band of men to assist in whatever tragedy or crisis had occured on the river, and in this instance about a half a dozen men came out to help pull the horse out of the unbearably cold water. They cut the tracers on the harness and hauled the beast out. This tough sturdy animal survived the ordeal because of its determined nature, says Archie. There was no way to get the horse back to its island home until the ice broke up and the river was clear, so they found a place for him in a neighbor's barn on the Canadian side.

There are no farms on the shores of the St. Lawrence Seaway now. No island communities, or neighborly exchanges on the river. Speed boats and snowmobiles have replaced the scows and cutters. "It was a real Shangri-La," boasts Archie of Mille Roches and the house in old Mille Roches where his mother raised ten children. It was a town that never really knew hard times, he says, because the Provincial Paper Mill provided jobs for many, and there was always a way for others to make a living if they wanted to. There was always a way to get by in Mille Roches. A way to get by on the river.

"My children will remember it the way it is now," he says, "but I'll always remember it the way it was."

There are bits and pieces of the Lost Villages still

evident along the Seaway—short stretches of road, misplaced sidewalks that lead out into the river, and the foundations of forgotten farm houses. But by far the best way to see many of the villages is by strapping a bottle of oxygen to your back. The inundation of the Lost Villages has created a strange mix of dry land and marine heritage.

In the early 1980s scuba divers began to ask the Lost Villages Historical Society about the villages, and about the remains that could still be seen under the St. Lawrence. Soon a relationship developed between the divers and this group of former residents which eventually led to the formation of a local chapter of a marine conservation organization known as Save Ontario Shipwrecks (SOS).

Like the Lost Villages, SOS-Ingleside is a strange mix. Made up of young sport divers and elderly and middle-aged residents of the villages, they use their various resources and knowledge to create underwater dive trails, and to foster a greater awareness of the archaeological and historical significance of the villages. They are committed to promoting and encouraging diving into the villages, and to protecting fragile or important archaeological sites from damage and illegal salvage.

Directions

Our tour of the Lost Villages begins on dry land, however, on the river shore at Mille Roches. From Cornwall take Highway 2 west to Guindon Park which is situated on the shore facing the submerged village.

This aerial photograph of Mille Roches was taken before the town disappeared under the waters of the St. Lawrence Seaway. Photo by Marcel Quenneville, courtesy of the S. D. & G. Historical Society, Inverarden Museum.

Mille Roches

It's been suggested that Mille Roches, or thousand rocks, was named because of the many rocks found at the head of a small set of rapids east of the village. This would have been named by French traders, but Fran Laflamme surmises that it was not the rapids the French were referring to but the abundance of fine quality limestone that was later quarried and used to build all the canals from Cornwall to Iroquois. This quarry was famous in the 19th century and certainly known in 18th century Quebec. Laflamme suggests that early requests to the King of France for assistance to develop a quarry at the Longue Sault is the reason it came to be called Mille Roches. The canal ruins at Iroquois are an excellent example of this limestone which was mistaken for and often called marble.

It's difficult to find evidence of this village on land but sport divers regularly explore and rediscover Mille Roches. The Power House has become one of the most popular dive sites in the area. Completed in 1901, it generated up to 3000 horsepower and provided electric power for two townships until it ceased operation in 1955. In 1958 a ball and crane demolished the building. What appears at first encounter to be just a pile of brick and rubble is in fact a dive trail, marked and easily accessible to divers new to the area. At 11 meters can be found the gate mechanisms and wheel chambers, at 16 meters on the powerhouse floor are the exciter reservoirs and Samson turbines, and at 23 meters the arched water release pit and tailrace.

To find the village today stand on the dock at Guindon Park and look south over the water — this is Mille Roches. A dive buoy is just barely visible in the distance—$1/2$ nautical mile—which marks the site of the power house.

To the left of the dock and not far from shore would be the Provincial Paper Mill which employed many and gave the town economic stability until construction of the Seaway forced it to move. Some archaeological work has been done at the paper mill. In time it may become a dive trail but at present diving on it is discouraged.

Moulinette

Now follow Highway 2 west to Lakeview Park which faces this lost village. It is documented that the Village of Moulinette was so named because of the many mills that operated there in the 1800s, *moulin* being the French word for mill.

The United Empire Loyalists who settled along the front tended to name the towns and villages after the homes they left, obvious landmarks or prominent members of the community and founding families. So we find places called Osnabruck, Woodlands, and Farran's Point. Why then would German, English, and Gaelic speaking people come to call this place Moulinette? There was no great influx of French families until after the turn of the century with the increase in heavy industry. Where did this French influence come from?

There was a significant French influence on the

St. Lawrence long before the grist and saw mills of Moulinette were built. French voyageurs are responsible for naming many sites along the river. Fran Laflamme, former president of the Lost Villages Historical Society, has also pondered this point and offers an alternative explanation. Perhaps it is not *moulin*, or mill, that is meant here, but the exact translation of *mounlinet* which is winch. Imagine, she says, the voyageurs with their large full-loaded bateaux confronted by the rapids and fast water of the Long Sault. It is possible that instead of unloading and portaging they might have winched their boats upriver and eventually named the site where this activity took place?

Whatever the origins of Moulinette's name, an 1850 account describes this village as having a grist mill with three run of stone, a saw mill, shingle factory, last factory, ashery, and two churches—the Episcopal and the Methodist. By the time the Seaway was constructed, Moulinette, like many rural Ontario villages affected by changes in agriculture and transportation, was declining, having at that time only a cheese factory and a few small businesses.

Above water the only traces of this village are a couple of strips of old pavement that once led out to the village. The entrance to Lakeview Park on Highway 2 was once the road to Moulinette. However, nautical relics near this riverfront community still exist, and SOS divers are doing archaeological work on the many wreck sites in the old canal east of Moulinette. To date they have found a dredge, two barges, and what appear to be a couple of tug boats.

There's much speculation as to the name and story behind the dredge, which is not a maintained and documented dive trail like the powerhouse, but lures sport divers just the same. Former residents can recall the dredge being inhabited at one time, and the crew's quarters were later used as a change house for canal skaters. At some point, perhaps when it was being used as a change house, the dredge burned to the water level and fell over into the canal. John Van Baal, president of SOS-Ingleside, believes the dredge may have been used during the renovation of the canal and the building of the dam and powerhouse at Mille Roches at the turn of the century.

The barges are of little interest to sport divers. "It isn't the kind of place you want to take tourist divers," says Van Baal. "It's silty and dark and there isn't a whole lot to see." But the historical and archaeological information found there could prove exciting.

Divers have also found what appear to be two tugs in the first Cornwall Canal (1840-1890). Partially salvaged, then abandoned, the tugs, like the barges, may have been used during canal renovations. Moulinette seems to have been a parking lot for vessels used in river and canal construction across Eastern Ontario. This kind of work slowed during the Depression and many of these vessels—like the tugs—were eventually abandoned.

Fittingly enough the village built to replace Mille Roches and Moulinette was named Long Sault (New

Town No. 2), for both villages were situated near the famous Long Sault Rapids.

Long Sault Rapids

There's no doubt that French Voyageurs named this Longue Sault, French for "long jump."

The site of the mighty Soo can be seen at Long Sault Rapids Point in the Long Sault Parkway. The location of this once fearsome stretch of river is not difficult. A strip of the old Highway 2 runs along the south side of this island, down into the river and back up again on a nearby island. The rapids are south of the old bit of highway.

Once seen as a major obstacle in the building of the Seaway, and an important source of future power for Ontario Hydro, the Rapids were stilled on 4 April 1957. Once tamed, they were reflooded on 11 December 1957.

According to Clive and Frances Marin in their work *Stormont, Dundas and Glengarry: 1945-1978*, the Rapids were silenced by building one pylon at the head of the Cornwall Canal and another on Long Sault Island. "Cables were strung between the two towers and small 'ship cans' began dumping up to 25 tons of rock into the water, thus slowly cutting of the Rapids." A few days prior to closing the rapids off behind the dam, the concentrated force of the stream had gained so much momentum that it swept the rocks away as they were dumped in.

The last house leaves Wales. This Ontario Hydro 1957 photo shows a Hartshorne house-mover transporting the last house from the old village of Wales to the new village of Ingleside. The machines lifted 200 ton houses with hydraulically controlled cables. Two houses could be moved a day under ideal conditions.
Photo courtesy S. D. & G. Historical Society, Inverarden Museum.

Eventually engineers developed the "hexapedian," an object made of welded girders with six steel legs. On the second attempt (at the first it was washed downstream), the hexapedian was dropped into the torrential gap. Boulders were quickly dumped on top of it; the gap narrowed. The Rapids were silenced.

Wales

The next stop on the Lost Villages route is Wales, so named following the visit of the Prince of Wales in 1860. Until that time it was not a town, simply the train station for Dickinson's Landing. Local histories tell a colorful tale of the devotion of the Prince's loyal subjects. Anticipating his arrival and not having a suitable red carpet to lay down, the women collected maple leaves and spread them out. It was this path of leaves that the Prince and his entourage followed out to the Landing where he was to board a steamer and shoot the rapids.

The village of Wales was the only inland village affected by the Seaway. The water is shallow here and you can wade through most of it if you are so inclined. The site of Wales can be seen from the Union Valley Cemetery on Highway 2 between Ingleside and Long Sault. The island directly in front of the Cemetery is the hill where St. David's Anglican church once stood. Three arched windows from this church have been installed in the Anglican church in Long Sault.

Divers seldom visit Wales because of the shallow water and the silt from Hoople Creek, but they did locate the old railway bridge which is still standing under the water. This was the first project undertaken by SOS-Ingleside at the request of the historical society. Residents knew that the bridge was one of the few structures left standing at the time of the flooding and were simply curious as to whether or not it was still there.

Van Baal was part of this first expedition to Wales and agrees that while it isn't a great dive site, standing on top of the bridge and feeling the current run through your hair instead of the wind is a moving example of the displacement divers often experience in the Lost Villages.

Wales at the time of the flooding was a pleasant little village surrounded by rolling hills, farms, and orchards. Several businesses operated there including a feedmill, a poultry farm, and an egg grading station.

Dickinson's Landing

From Wales, follow the Long Sault Parkway west to a dive marker just offshore near MacDonell Island. This is the site of another Lost Village, Dickinson's Landing.

Barnabas Dickenson was responsible for establishing the first stage and steamer mail service between Montreal and Kingston shortly after the War of 1812. Except for a slight change in spelling, this stopping place on the river continued to bear

Lock 21, Dickinson's Landing, as shown in this 1920 postcard, is now under 20 meters of water. Photo courtesy of the S. D. & G. Historical Society, Inverarden Museum (86-21.25).

the name Dickinson's Landing. Before his river service, sporadic dispatches were made by foot through the bush. Deliveries could sometimes take several months. Barnabas died of cholera in Cornwall in 1832.

The village is the site of the most popular and extensive dive trail in the Seaway, and attracts divers from across Canada and the U.S. It is here at Lock 21 that many divers begin their love affair with the Lost Villages. More than one diver has said it's as if the lock master just picked up his things and walked away when he saw the flood water coming. The lock house is gone but almost everything else is as it was in July 1958. Under 20 meters of water divers can find handrails, motors, and the cables and gears used to get the lakers up the river. The canal walls, built of stone from the quarry at Mille Roches, can also be explored.

A dive marker can be seen just off shore on MacDonell Island on the Long Sault Parkway. A dive line runs out from this marker to Lock 21; the village was west of the Locks.

In the 1800s the landing was a booming little community, the stopping place for much of the river traffic. But with the development of inland roads and the decline of river traffic, it had shrunk considerably at the time of the flooding. During the 1940s and 1950s the town dock was the center of activity. Cream was loaded onto boats and shipped to Montreal, coal to supply the township of Osnabruck was delivered and stored in the coal shed behind Ransom's store, and a ferry service stopped here. The town boasted a post office, Bullock's Hotel, Our

Lady of Grace Catholic Church, and a cheese factory with a butcher shop on one end that delivered several times a week. The light house from the Landing has been moved to Upper Canada Village where it can be seen today.

Woodlands and Santa Cruz

Following the Long Sault Parkway, we come to Woodlands and Santa Cruz. The origins of these hamlets are lost in time. Woodlands simply may have been a heavily wooded section of the river. Santa Cruz offers more to the imagination. A local myth is sometimes told but seldom heeded of Portuguese sailors who somehow made it up the river and stayed long enough to name a stopping place. But this is purely myth as no evidence or documentation corroborates the story.

These small clusters of houses and farms along old Highway 2 were remnants of early United Empire Loyalist settlements that never really grew into full fledged towns. Tourist cottages and the private cottages of locals from along the Front could be found on this section of the river, as could a church and a few small businesses, many catering to the tourist trade.

Any bits and pieces that remain of Santa Cruz are in the Long Sault Parkway. Woodlands lies today between the village of Ingleside and Croil Island. The oldest court records for Lunenburg (the name given to the whole of Eastern Ontario in the late 1700s) show that the first session in the district was held at

Woodlands in June 1789. A man convicted of assault and battery was imprisoned until he could pay his one shilling fine. Fifteen months later in the same court a man was sentence to "39 lashes on the naked back" for petty larceny. His female accomplice was pardoned.

Farran's Point

Our next stop is Farran's Point, just west of Ingleside, one of the new villages (New Town No. 1) like Long Sault created for the displaced citizens of Dickinson's Landing, Farran's Point, Wales, and Aultsville.

Information on the origins of the name Farran's Point are sketchy but it is safe to assume it was named for the Farran family who were early settlers here. The biggest social attraction at "The Point" was Lock 22 and the open air pavilion. Warm summer nights and Sunday afternoons were spent picnicking, watching the lakers being locked, and feeding coins into the nickelodeon. This pavilion, where couples once danced to the hits of the 1930s and 1940s, can be found today at the Fairgrounds in Newington.

The closest you can get to "The Point" by car is Farran Park at Ingleside. Mrs. Sheets' pines in front of the parking lot are the last traces of her home east of the village. Old photos from the 1920s and 1930s show the pines standing there then.

A tour by boat reveals Farran's Point Road running down into the river southwest of the park. Like Wales, the village is in the shallows, and in late summer many of the streets are dry, and by early winter, when the mud flats are frozen, you can walk down the sidewalks. Many foundations and other clues that people once lived here are becoming overgrown with trees and shrubs as the shoreline gradually reverts to a more natural state.

"The southwest corner of the campgrounds at Farran Park is a stone's throw away from the approach wall of Lock 22," says Van Baal. It's an interesting dive and warrants further investigation, he says, because both the old lock and the new lock constructed in the early 1900s are in reasonably good shape, but because of a strong current it's not as popular as Lock 21.

It's here that divers are searching for the wreck of an Aultsville-Louisville Landing ferry. Milk, cream, automobiles, and, it is rumored, bootleg beer were ferried across the river to the American side during Prohibition. A former resident has given fairly detailed directions to the wrecked ferry but it has so far eluded divers.

There was a bay east of the village and here lies the Graveyard Point Wreck. It was in this bay that ice was cut before homes were equipped with refrigerators. Van Baal believes this barge, loaded with stone, was once a schooner converted to a barge after the decline of wind-powered vessels. Like the wrecks in the old canal near Moulinette, more information is needed for positive identification.

Aultsville

Formerly Charlesville, this village was named to honor Samuel Ault, Member of the Legislative Assembly from 1861 to 1867, and Member of Parliament from 1867 to 1872. The Ault family were prominent citizens of this community and were proprietors of several businesses, including a saw mill, a general store, and a logging operation.

There was a time when the communities along the front depended heavily on the river for their livelihood. Dickinson's Landing depended on river travel, Moulinette needed river power to generate the mills, and Aultsville, too, flourished because of the river.

Four Irish potters saw the potential of the river here and by 1851 the Elliott brothers were plying their craft in Aultsville. Two of these brothers bought land and went on to become well-known businessmen. William operated the pottery factory and John the brickyard and small pottery.

John and William's factories have become important archaeological sites. In 1987 two provincial archaeologists and divers from SOS-Ingleside began an expedition to find the Aultsville potteries. The expedition proved successful. Divers found what appeared to be a factory dump in the old river bed. A broken crock with the traditional strap handle was found, as were other bits of pottery and bricks. These discoveries, coupled with clay samples from the bottom of the river, enabled archaeologists to document the potteries for the first time.

While great-grandmother's fine porcelain dishes

would have been imported, chances are good that if she lived along the Front, her pickle crock and bean jar were from the Aultsville potteries. Because so much of the redware produced at the potteries was not marked, it is often hard to identify it positively and this has caused considerable debate among collectors and antique dealers.

If there's one thing locals agree upon, it's that Aultsville was a very pretty place. Towering trees lined the streets and framed the grand brick houses that in the end were knocked to the ground. Because, with a few exceptions, only frame houses were moved to the new towns of Ingleside and Long Sault, much of John Elliott's legacy has also disappeared.

The Garlough house—now Cooks Tavern at Upper Canada Village—came from west of Aultsville and is one of the few brick houses to survive the construction of the Seaway.

For reasons of conservation, sport diving is discouraged and closely monitored at the pottery sites as additional archaeological work has yet to be done. When the water is low you can walk out to Aultsville. A one kilometer strip of old pavement as you enter the Upper Canada Bird Sanctuary is part of the Aultsville Road. A gate prevents traffic from driving down the hill and over the old railway track but on foot you can find at the water's edge the sidewalks of this once very pretty village.

Mary "Granny Hoople" Whitmore Hoople, 1767-1858. Photo courtesy of E.L. Hoople, author of *The Hooples of Hoople's Creek.*

Hoople's Creek

The mouth of Hoople's Creek, now altered by the St. Lawrence Seaway, was the site of an early United Empire Loyalist settlement and home to a woman whose intelligence, courage, and gift of healing saved the lives of many of the first European settlers in Stormont County.

It was here on the Hoople that several German farmers took up the land grants they received as members of Sir John Johnson's British force, the King's Royal Regiment of New York. After facing defeat against the revolutionaries in the American War of Independence, Johnson and the Royal Greens fled north and finally made their way to what is today Eastern Ontario. They arrived a tired and defeated people, and with sparse provisions and tools began the daunting task of cutting away the trees and clearing the land. By 1788 the families at the Hoople settlement—named for brothers Henry and John Hoople of the Royal Greens—were very close to starvation.

The British were less than generous with provisions and supplies for these farming families. Unlike other Loyalist settlements, the people of the Hoople and those along the St. Lawrence did not receive ploughs, lumber, brick, or even nails to begin building their new homes. What tools they were given to break new ground were limited indeed. They received coarse cloth and blankets for pants and coats, and boots they fashioned either from cloth or animal hide. Each family was given seed wheat, one hand saw, and a short handled axe like those used on ships, which the farmers found virtually useless for felling trees. A whip saw and cross-cut saw were to be shared between two families, and a set of tools—chisels, auger, drawknive—and one fire-lock were to be shared between five families. The small number of livestock that arrived later to be shared by five families was not sufficient to go around.

These people relied on nothing but their own hard labor. Because they had to wait for lumber and grist mills to be built, raising livestock and putting up adequate barns would take several years.

They had little time to establish themselves in their new home when severe weather and crop failure resulted in the infamous "hungry year" (1788). It is little wonder that the people of the Hoople were in a sorry state when eighteen-year-old Mary Whitmore arrived. Settlers along the river were already trading what little they had for food. Two hundred acre lots were bartered for a few pounds of flour, and a good cow for eight bushels of potatoes. Those with nothing to trade were eating wild leeks, tree buds, and leaves.

Mary Whitmore came to the Hoople in a voyageur canoe loaded with fur. She had lost the ability to speak both the German and English languages of her parents for she had spent the past seven years as the adopted daughter of a Delaware medicine woman. All contact with her family had been lost, save for her mother's German brother who had settled on the Hoople.

Mary was the only member of the Whitmore family with whom Mary's uncle, Jacob Sheets, had been able to make contact since he first heard of the massacre at Chillisquaque Creek on the Pennsylvanian frontier. The family farm had been raided by a mixed band of Indian and American revolutionaries. Several children, including Mary, had been taken hostage by the Indians; her parents and two of their other children had been murdered, and the fate of three more children, who had been tending the fires in the sugar bush, was never determined.

Mary had the gift of healing. This proved to be a valuable asset for the settlers on the Hoople, but in the years that followed the "hungry winter" she also applied her Delaware teachings to find food in the forest along the river. Had it not been for this woman many in the settlement would have starved.

Following her marriage to Henry Hoople she continued to be the settlement's only doctor, using her Native herbal medicines, inherent gift of healing, and incredible courage and intelligence to treat the people of the settlement.

Eventually school-trained physicians began to establish themselves along the Front, but it appears Mary gained the respect of those learned men just as she had gained the respect of the settlers, for she continued to practice. Granny Hoople, as she is known locally, raised eleven of her twelve children to adulthood, an amazing accomplishment in the late 1700s, and lived to be ninety-one years old.

Descendants bearing the Hoople surname are rare along the Front now. There is little doubt, however, that many of the German Loyalist names still common—Rombough, Shaver, Wert, and Empey, to list a very few—if not directly linked to the Hooples of Hoople Creek, are still heard today because of

Granny Hoople's healing hands. She attended the births of many of Osnabruck Township's early residents, and healed them of a multitude of ailments and injuries.

Most of the first settlement on the Hoople is now under the waters of the St. Lawrence Seaway, but Mary Whitmore Hoople's home can still be found on the second concession of Osnabruck Township. At the United Counties Museum in Cornwall, Granny Hoople's bowl, which held the gilead salve she used to soothe the complaints of her patients, can be seen. Five Hoople tombstones, including Mary's, are part of the Loyalist Memorial at Upper Canada Village.

Morrisburg

Conveniently located on the St. Lawrence River navigation system, Morrisburg was home to a number of riverboat captains. Incorporated in 1860, the village soon ranked as one of Ontario's wealthiest. Growth was rapid, and by 1878 the town boasted 2,000 inhabitants, rivalling Cornwall in size.

The transhipment center for Dundas County's burgeoning dairy industry, Morrisburg attracted a steel-rolling mill which employed 300 people in 1908, and was an important part of the town's industrial base. When this industry relocated to Hamilton, Challies' Dental Products—the makers of the first toothbrush in Canada—began production in 1917. In turn, Challies' was bought by George

Main Street, Morrisburg, 1949 — before the flooding.
Reeve George Beavers said that it "was a great day
for Canadians and Canada" when he learned that
the Seaway was going to be built.
Photo courtesy S. D. & G. Historical Society,
Inverarden Museum.

Beavers who transformed his dental products business into one of North America's largest and became the village's principal employer.

As a result of the flooding of the Seaway it was projected that 1/3 of the town would be submerged, including the entire business district. Ontario Hydro offered to set up the displaced merchants in a new shopping center. Forty of the village's fifty businesses accepted the offer. But — with the notable exception of Beavers Dental Products — most industry simply didn't relocate and Morrisburg's subsequent growth was capped.

Upper Canada Playhouse, Morrisburg

After several years' of production at the temporary tent theater on Upper Canada Road, the Upper Canada Playhouse finally found a permanent home in the village of Morrisburg. The old Odonto toothbrush factory, west of the traffic lights and across from the water tower on Highway 2, was feverishly transformed in the spring of 1990 and officially became the property of the Playhouse in early 1991. Productions begin in June and continue into early September; however, the new location may allow management to extend the season. The Playhouse usually offers a varied selection of shows each season including musicals, comedy, and drama. Ticket and schedule information can be obtained by writing to the playhouse.

Story

Lucien, the Acadian mill worker, doesn't dress like Marshall Button or talk like Marshall Button. In fact, Lucien appears to be several inches shorter and at least 10 pounds heavier than the man who portrays him. But when the lights go down and the night shift at the pulp and paper mill begins, a character emerges who is so convincing you understand immediately why Marshall Button has developed an identity problem.

"I'm not Lucien," the artistic director of the Upper Canada Playhouse in Morrisburg says of the character he has created. But summer theater audiences, who continue to fill the house each season, aren't always sensitive to that.

There really is a guy named Lucien who drinks too much, smokes too much, and dreams of winning the lottery so he won't have to come to work any more.

"He says things that I would never say," Button laments of the character who at times he has no control over. When writing new material and updating the show this writer\actor\director can look at things objectively, but on stage Lucien takes over. "If someone in the audience yells something, Marshall doesn't answer, Lucien does."

Actors and writers strive to create such a character, one that is genuine and has its own voice, but because of this Button is quick to point out that the opinions of the character are not his. Button is just as quick to come to Lucien's defence. "He says these things out of innocence, not ignorance." Both character

Actor-Director Marshall Button as 'Lucien,' performing at the Upper Canada Playhouse, Morrisburg. Photo by Dan Pritchard, courtesy of Upper Canada Playhouse.

and creator call Dalhousie on New Brunswick's North Shore home.

Sometimes when the show is over and the lights go on, members of the audience still have a problem with Button's true identity. He tells of an experience he had while performing the show in Prince George, a pulp and paper town in northern British Columbia. The fragrance of the mill was so strong you could smell it even inside the theater and evidently much of the audience was made up of mill workers not unlike Lucien himself. Within ten seconds of the curtain call a man who had been sitting in the front row jumped up on stage and began telling Lucien that he was from Atholville, New Brunswick, about 25 kilometers from Dalhousie. In rapid French he introduced himself and his wife and wanted to know who Lucien's people were. He wanted to know Lucien's last name in case he knew the family.

"I was trying to tell him my mother-in-law was from Atholville . . . I was trying to tell him my name was Marshall Button but it didn't click. He was just so excited and keen. He had seen this guy from home who worked in a mill. That's all it was."

Lucien is just a guy from home, whether you see him in Prince George, or Timmins, or Dalhousie. We all know a man who has the same qualities and short-comings, and that's why local audiences keep coming back, and why Button continues to travel the country with Lucien, introducing live theater to people who normally would not be experiencing it. People like Lucien, people like the Prince George mill worker whose family is from Atholville.

Though Lucien and Marshall Button may have an

identity problem, the much-debated and discussed Canadian identity is far from ambiguous for Button. Because of Lucien's popularity, the show has been performed in all but two provinces over the last decade and many of these performances have been in small northern centers where Button is treated like a visiting relative. These visits, particularly the ones in the north, have convinced him that a wonderful sense of humor has evolved among these people because of the cold and the hard life they live. "It's a shame," he says. "With all the things dividing this country . . . the more you travel, the more you think they are different, the more you really see they're the same. Northern British Columbia is like Northern New Brunswick and nobody can tell me any different."

Lucien can be heard echoing similar sentiments and suggests protests and demonstrations in the middle of a Canadian winter tend to put things in the proper prospective. "Not too much I change wit' Canada," says the Maritimer. "We lucky us. Got a problem wit' somebody? Jus' go stand outside for couple 'our in January."

While too modest to admit that Lucien, in spite of his sometimes narrow views and lack of sophistication, is wise, Button does believe that the personal tragedies this character endures are the reason the show works as well as it does. Lucien is uproariously funny, and while we may laugh at his fear that his estranged wife and two children may be lured into Protestantism up in the big city of Fredericton, the pain of a failed marriage is not lost in the laughter. Lucien is able to laugh at himself, at his church, at his country, and this is a trait that his creator admires in him. It is also a trait that they share.

"*I'm an Acadian,*" *says Marshall Button.* "*My father is a Newfoundlander but my mother is an Acadian, which probably has a lot to do with what I do for a living. The two groups of people who were poked fun at where I grew up were Newfoundlanders and French Canadians. So I had to learn to be funnier than everyone else. Or at least know all the jokes so I could ruin their punch lines.*"

Old Author's Farm

To reach our next destination, turn south at the Highway 31 intersection in Morrisburg. Travel south to Gibson Lane which is identified by a sandwich board sign north of the municipal dock. You have now arrived at the Old Author's Farm.

Nancy Edmonds and husband Duncan are the proprietors of the Old Author's Farm, an old and rare book store with an illustrious past.

If you're not a book collector, they could turn you into one. If you are a collector or the kind of person who shivers with delight at the sight of wall to wall, ceiling to floor books, you can count on them to have something to add to your shelves at home.

The Edmonds didn't set out to buy an antique book store, although they had entertained the idea a time or two during their forty years of book collecting. They began as customers. One day, while rummaging through the more than 4,000 books at the Old Author's Farm, the desire to own a store of their own hit them again and they decided to ask the owners if they were interested in selling the place. They were, and the Old Author's Farm changed hands.

It's clear from the fond respect with which Nancy speaks that they aspire to maintain the reputation of the shop and the man who first established it. Old Author's began in Ottawa in the 1930s, and its founder, Borden Clarke, catered to many prestigious and meticulous clients, including Louis St. Laurent, Sir Winston Churchill, and Franklin D. Roosevelt. He moved the shop out to Morrisburg in the late 1950s, and after more than four decades in the business Clarke sold that store in 1974, but stayed on as consultant until shortly before his death. Over the course of his career, Clarke, who came to be known as "the old author" although he had never written a book, dealt not only with important people but with historic papers and documents as well. He bought and sold Louis Riel's last letter, and saved Colonel John By's first hand drawn maps of the Rideau Canal from being consigned to the dustbin.

Being a book dealer is more than simply buying and then selling at profit. It is detective work, and rescue work, and at times an incredibly exciting treasure hunt. You never know what you're going to find or where you're going to find it.

Some requests seem hopelessly impossible. Like the man who wanted a copy of the primer he had used in a one-room prairie school house. It seemed like a long shot, says Nancy, but she promised to keep an eye out for it. Not long after her conversation with the sentimental school boy she attended a book show in the U.S.A. and, just in case, visited a children's book exhibit. She shakes her head in amazement—there was the book. A hunt like that might have taken years.

As well as looking after clients who have come to depend on Old Author's for rare and out of prints books, the Edmonds are working to expand and improve the various buildings that make up the farm. A humble Victorian working-man's cottage has been renovated; in keeping with the period, this tiny dwelling has been filled with 19th century furnishings and literature. Here customers are encouraged to sit a while and relax, enjoy a cup of tea perhaps, and look over the wonderful literary treasures they may have found.

G.E.

Directions

Our next tour begins in the north of Stormont and Dundas Counties, in "Apple-Cheddar" country. You may choose to pick up the "Apple-Cheddar Route" by taking Highway 31 north to Dundela (home of the McIntosh Apple) and Winchester (the cheese capital of Ontario). Or you may choose to return to Cornwall and Montreal via Highway 401 east, to Kingston and Toronto via the west bound lanes.

CHAPTER 7

The Apple-Cheddar Route

Preamble

I hope you are hungry because when you set out on this route you are going to discover enough fresh cheese and home grown apples to satisfy the largest appetites. The rolling hills and well-tended farms of greater north Stormont and Dundas Counties are the home of the McIntosh apple and the Canadian Holstein cow. Nestled along Highway 43 and the various county roads you will discover picturesque villages and hamlets which hold the key to the origins of our world famous dairy industry. You will see enough romantic Victorian architecture to take you back to another era, and visit Williamsburg, the home of Dr. Locke the 'foot' fixer. The downhome stories related by oral historian Clarence Cross will make the past come alive. In fact there is so much to find that when the five members of the Tri-County Writers' and I set out one day in two cars to explore the countryside, we were quickly overwhelmed with the wealth of natural and man made heritage.

The Apple-Cheddar route outlined here is only one of a number of possible trips you might take through this part of Eastern Ontario. To fit this trip into one day, I've selected a few interesting shops, but have had to by-pass other equally historic and colorful areas, such as the villages of Avonmore, Berwick, Finch, Moose Creek, and South Mountain. I have, I hope, alerted you to the possibilities, and invite you to wander from our route to discover these communities another day.

I.B.

History

What could be more Canadian than apples and cheddar cheese? While the United Counties may not have a monopoly on cheddar, Dundela in Dundas County can claim to be the home of the McIntosh apple.

Rural in nature, the landscape on this route is dotted by numerous small farming villages and farms that are often home to the Holstein cow, first introduced to Canada here. The area's most famous citizen was Dr. Mahlon W. Locke, the 'foot' fixer of Williamsburgh. Able to cure arthritis with his famous twist of the foot, Dr. Locke, a modest country physician,

THE APPLE-CHEDDAR ROUTE

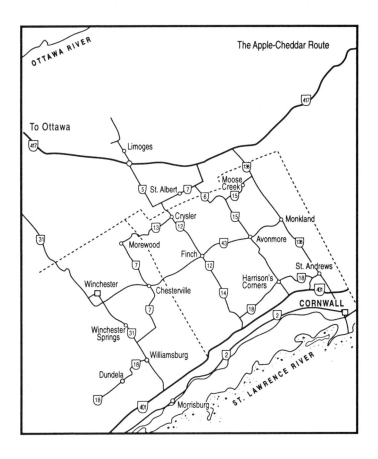

achieved international acclaim before the Second World War.

Driving through the countryside you will see numerous low concrete buildings at nearly every crossroad village. Now largely abandoned, these buildings were once cheese factories that processed the dairy products from the surrounding farms, and often provided the much needed cash to bridge the gap between profit and loss on the many family farms.

Centered in the County town of Cornwall, the Cornwall Cheese and Butter Board was formed in 1898. Growing rapidly, the 38 Board members sold $60,000 worth of dairy products a week, making it the largest cash industry in Cornwall and the Counties by 1919. The largest dairy industry in Canada, with 2,000 milk producers, or patrons as they were known, the board's suppliers came from across the three counties. With no membership fees, the Cornwall Board was "acknowledged by experts in the dairy industry to be the best conducted and most loyal" in the Dominion. By loyal, they meant that there were no 'curb' sales, and that the board had a monopoly on all the cheese sold locally.

Producing cheddar, the board was based on the factory system which started in New York State around 1851. The system was introduced to the United Counties in 1867 by De Bellefeuille MacDonald at his Gray's Creek estate.

The system spread rapidly and turned cheese production from a casual pastime to a profitable export industry. Initially run by individuals, and sometimes operated as partnerships, these enterprises evolved into joint stock companies organized to make cheese, butter, and profits efficiently.

A company's capital would be divided into small shares to permit more shareholders. These milk suppliers, known as 'patrons,' would supplement their capital with funds from non-suppliers known as 'drys.' Profits and operating costs accrued from the fee charged by the proprietor to the patron for production. In cooperative ventures, the shareholders might be paid dividends.

Every Monday at 2 p.m. exactly, the moment of truth (and profit) arrived when the President of the Board invited buyers from eight of Canada's leading cheese companies to start bidding for the week's produce, listed on the blackboard in Cornwall's Town Hall.

After World War I, the system began to suffer some cracks with Kraft purchasing a cheese factory in Newington in 1936. In 1940 the Counties still counted 150 small cheese factories and creameries, but by 1978 there were only three large factories left, and only one produced cheddar.

Some people who remember the rapid demise of the factories blame Kraft and the process of centralization. To do so ignores the fact that Britain, one of the largest purchasers of cheddar, could not afford Canadian cheese after World War II. It fails to take into consideration the costs of modernization in the face of more stringent health regulations, and large scale competition from Ault and Borden's. Whatever the reason for the passing of the factory system, cheese is still produced locally. In 1970 Kraft

Ingleside had 200 people on the payroll throughout the Counties, and financed the growth of Thompson Transport, a local trucking firm. By 1990 Kraft had become a major local employer with 400 people working at the Ingleside plant. Sadly for fresh cheese curd lovers, curds—once a local delicacy and revived for a short time at Upper Canada Village—are no longer made here since the Health Board closed down the Village's 19th century operation because it did not meet modern Health codes. All, however, is not lost, and in the tradition of the Glengarrians, who appropriate other geographical areas if they feel the need, we are fortunate to have St. Albert Cheese in nearby Russell County to supply the demand.

Directions

Our tour of Apple-Cheddar country begins just north of Dundas County at St. Albert. From Ottawa, take Highway 417 south to the exit for Limoges and follow the signs south to St. Albert. From Cornwall, take Highway 138 north to Stormont County Road 15 leading to Moose Creek; from Moose Creek take County Road 15 northwest to Road 6, then turn left at 7 to St. Albert. Be on the look out for cattle crossings.

St. Albert

Plan to arrive in St. Albert in time for a fresh batch of curds at 10 a.m. any day of the week at the local cheese factory. Old curds just don't cut it with true curd lovers. They must be squeaky fresh!

This is a Franco-Ontarian area of the province, a world of "fromagiers" or cheesemakers who have often learned the skill from their forefathers. Courses are taught in agricultural colleges, too. Customers get to view the cheesemaking process from start to finish, and can question the retail outlet employees, trying out their sometimes fractured French in the bargain. In Eastern Ontario, where cheese factories are no longer found in every town and village as they once were, St. Albert's survives because of a local passion for fresh cheddar. Here, cheddar curds are eaten in "poutine," a treat amounting to a meal, which consists of a generous portion of French fries and curds smothered in gravy. It's an acquired taste, as was pointed out to me by a Scot. I was quick to remind him that haggis is an acquired taste for most of us, too! Whether you eat your curds in the car on the way home as most do, or wait to eat them with potato chips in front of the TV, you'll soon be back to St. Albert, Fresh Curd Capital of Eastern Ontario since 1894.

Story

Milk and milk products have been an important part of the diet of residents of the United Counties since the early settlement days when simple farm cheeses were made by women from surplus milk. An extract from the stomach of young calves called rennet enabled the cheesemaker to separate the curds and whey to make various cheeses. The United Empire Loyalists are credited with bringing the art of cheesemaking on a large scale to Ontario. The actual factory system dates from 1864 when a certain Harvey Farrington of New York settled in North Norwich and built his cheese factory there. By 1888 the cheddar cheese process had become common. Before this, granular or stirred curd cheeses had been the norm. Cheddar, which originated in Cheddar, Somerset, England, has become the preferred cheese in North America, and the residents of the United Counties consume vast amounts of it.

The largest wheel of cheese ever manufactured, known as the "Canadian Mite," was made in Perth in Eastern Ontario. Our family proudly tells the story of a great-great grandfather who had the honor of accompanying it to the Chicago World's Fair in 1892. The wheel weighed 22,000 lbs., was 6 feet in height, and used the daily milk of 10,000 cows and 2 days' curd from 12 factories. The cheese caused a sensation when it broke through the floor while on display, and another when it was tasted by Sir Thomas Lipton, from England, who purchased it and judged it to be of excellent quality.

When the last factory in the United Counties closed in the 1970s, it signalled the end of a century of local cheesemaking. D.M. McPherson (1847-1915) was a giant in the industry. He developed it from the 1870s so that a cheese factory was within easy driving distance of every farmer in Glengarry. In 1871, the census reports two cheese factories only in Glengarry, but in 1909 The Glengarry News stated that there were now 77 factories operating in the county. McPherson, 'the

Cheese King,' and others had achieved great results, changing the agricultural picture of the area and creating a growing body of consumers for their product.

We have fond memories of our weekly visits to the cheese factory in Apple Hill during the 1960s. Outside, farmers off-loaded milk in cans into a cool underground cellar to the north of the building. Inside, one could watch the various stages of cheesemaking. Vast quantities of milk were heated to the prescribed temperature at which point rennet would be added. Later we watched the cheesemaker cut the curds with a wire contraption. As the curds cooked, he tested them periodically. Those who coveted warm curds waited impatiently for them to be washed and weighed. We had a passion for aged cheddar and waited to watch the pressing state. Mild or strong cheddar, both were enjoyed by locals at all hours of the day, but especially with an ale after a day's work on the farm. Souvenirs of that era of local cheesemaking are found all over the United Counties. They include the huge milk cans, now often humbled as umbrella stands or bar stools, and the wooden cheese hoops and boxes. Who can remember buying the great wheels of cheddar to last a whole winter? Who knows what cheese rind is today?

E.M.

Chesterville

The next stop on the route is Chesterville. From St. Albert take County Road 7 west to the intersection with County Road 12. Take this road south through

Crysler and Berwick to Finch, then turn west on Highway 43 to Chesterville. If you have the time, pause in the lovely villages of Crysler, Berwick, and Finch—all picturesque farming communities.

As you come off Highway 43 just over the bridge on Main Street you'll see an Imperial Gas Station. This site was once a blacksmith shop owned by Tophile Larbre. Next to it is the Chesterville and District Heritage Center which was originally the Township Hall for Winchester Township.

Besides being a Township Hall, this Heritage Center has changed character many times over the years. It was a movie theater, a fire hall, and a court house complete with holding cells whose occupants were never in a hurry to leave. This was because on cinema night they got to see a free silent film with a man named Jack Morris playing accompaniment on the piano. During World War I the building was a drill hall and the drillmaster a seventeen-year old farm boy whose only experience was canal duty on the St. Lawrence River the year before.

Across the street the community hall and parking lot sit where the old village square used to be. On the west side are two buildings that were once stores. Chesterville's earliest settlers came from the St. Lawrence area and built their first houses and businesses along the riverbank, now called Mill Street. The South Nation River, originally the Petite Nation, was the power source for the mills, and before the roads were built it provided transportation. Chesterville, the first place to be developed in North Dundas, was the most important center for several decades.

The McCloskey Hotel in Chesterville is located on Victoria Street, across from the old village square, where gentlemen sat on the now absent veranda, and ladies reclined on the balcony. Photo by Ian Bowering.

Next, travel to 25 Mill Street where the first settler, George Hummel, built his shanty. Bushland stood on both sides of the river when Hummel bought it in the early 1800s from descendants of Captain Richard Duncan, a United Empire Loyalist who lived at Mariatown. Hummel built his barns where St. Andrew's Presbyterian Church, erected in the 1880s, now stands. Later he constructed this frame house which has since been modernized. Here on the sidewalk would have been George's front yard and the spot where the first elections were held for the north part of Dundas County.

Story

Elections in the 1800s were held over a period of five successive days and were entertaining events. Here's how local historian and genealogist Clarence Cross describes the polling process:

It would be typically set up with trestle tables on one side of his front yard, by the Conservative candidate, loaded down with food and drink of various kinds, meats, cheeses, bread, ale and whisky and on the opposite side would be similar trestle tables, set up by the Reform candidate, also laden with all kinds of goodies. The candidates would be in full view making speeches and twisting arms with their supporters. The voting was open with everyone announcing his vote in a loud voice so there was much intimidation sometimes ending in fights. There was a lot of drunkenness which was characteristic of those days. Some of the men who couldn't make up their minds went from one side to the other sampling the wares of one candidate then sampling the wares of the other candidate and of course they would end up in the gutter somewhere.

Farther on down Mill Street the present day feed mill stands on the same site as the earliest one. Around 1830 Thomas Armstrong and his son built the first mill. It was a saw mill which he operated successfully for years. Then he sold the mills—there were now more than one—to John Flynn Crysler for the enormous sum of £3000. The average building in Chesterville at that time brought about £50. Other businesses set up operations in the same area, and with a shingle mill, a carding and pulling mill, and an iron foundry, this waterfront became the town's industrial section.

If you move on to 8 College Street you'll find a brick house so typical of the farmhouse style of the old days that it has been called the Ontario Farm House. Notice its L-shaped pattern with the half wrap-around veranda. Upstairs there is a large gable with two windows facing the street, and a smaller gable with a single window. The original windows have been replaced with energy-efficient ones, minus the original decorative features.

The little house opposite the public school, number 28, is one of Chesterville's oldest buildings. You can tell by the eave returns and the windows in the gable. At one time it was called McGinley's Hotel, and the Catholic priest stayed here when he came from Morrisburg to perform weddings and baptisms.

This was before the 1880s when the priests first arrived to live in Chesterville.

Turn and walk up Victoria Street, past a fine old house that was once a doctor's residence. By now you will be nearing the Heritage Center again, and a large brick building which at the turn of the century was a highly respectable establishment, the McCloskey Hotel. Note the Empire style mansard roof. You can see marks on the brick where front porches existed, and where a door once opened onto the upstairs terrace. Local raconteur Clarence Cross recalls, "My mother remembers well-dressed gentlemen sitting on the now absent downstairs veranda chewing tobacco, aiming at the spittoons near their feet, and swapping stories while the ladies reclined on the balcony above reading or talking quietly, at a distance from the men's coarse jocularity." You can't rent rooms here any more but the spartan bar is open.

Walk past the gas station onto Main Street where you will find St. Mary's Catholic School. Stroll down to a large grassy area where there used to be a cemetery. Find a stone that says "*George Hummel born 1821.*" He was the son of the original George Hummel. The three smaller stones around it commemorate other pioneers of the community. There's another graveyard, the oldest one, a few hundred yards down on the south side of the river but it was destroyed by a cyclone. If you look carefully, maybe you can find some remains of it.

As you walk back up Main Street you'll see St. Mary's Catholic Church built of local limestone in 1851. The magnificent church rectory is across the street. Beside the Catholic school is the convent

The Hummel Family's tombstone is located in the cemetery behind St. Mary's Catholic Church, Chesterville. Photo by Ian Bowering.

used in later years by the Sisters of Providence who came here from Kingston to teach. The concrete bridge you cross was built about 1950, replacing an earlier bridge constructed of iron trusses, and two previous wooden bridges.

The Main and King Street area was the old financial district. Fire destroyed it at the turn of the century but it was rebuilt. Louis' Restaurant used to be a bank in a block that housed a clothing store, a grocery store, and an upstairs where Hall's Music Store carried on a profitable business. Since these King Street stores had no plumbing, there was a row of outhouses in the alley behind them. On Hallowe'en night these outside water closets would find their way to the town square or be piled on the iron truss bridge along with buggies, and sleighs, and peoples' porch steps. The next morning you'd see the store owners trying to locate their own privies before they opened shop.

Locate Water Street and Trinity United Church, a beautiful Romanesque style building. The Church was under construction at the time of the fire and is different from anything you see in the area. The Centennial house at 34 Water Street is the original home of the Casselman family. Adventurous young James Casselman went to the California Gold rush to make his fortune. It seems that he didn't, so he came back and settled down to farming here in this old house built before 1860. His son Willie made a trip out to Victoria, British Columbia, saw a house he liked, returned, and built this cobblestone structure around 1917 from local fieldstone.

Find the corner of King and Queen Streets

where you can look across at a building with a boomtown front. This was the old Episcopal Methodist Church which later housed a coffin maker's business.

Walking on to 86 King Street you'll see a large Queen Anne style house, the only designated heritage building in Chesterville. It and the one immediately to the north were built in 1904 by two sisters. One sister married a doctor, and the other a merchant. The doctor's house, the heritage house, has a front entrance into his living quarters and a side entrance into his office. Though the sisters both married well, the doctor—who was a good doctor but a poor bill collector—had to give up his house and move to another more modest one. But the merchant was better at keeping accounts and collecting bills, so his house stayed in the family for two or three generations.

Continue to the corner of Macmillan and King Streets to the railway overlooking the Nestlés plant. The railroad, built in 1886 by the Ontario and Quebec Railway, was later controlled by the Canadian Pacific Railway. It allowed farmers in the area to ship their produce directly to market in Montreal, instead of taking it by wagon to Morrisburg and shipping it on the Grand Trunk Railway. The last passenger train went through here in the 1960s. The last remnant of the old railway is the circular stone water tower that had a wooden top which burned and was replaced by a cement one.

On the south side of the tracks where the station used to be is the site of the old Nestlés condensery where the farmers' milk was made into

Dr. Ellis' house, at 86 King Street, Chesterville, was constructed in 1904 in the Queen Anne style. The side entrance leads to the office, the front door was used by the family. Photo by Ian Bowering.

condensed and evaporated milk. It began as a farmers co-op but at the end of World War I Nestlés, which had West Indian markets, took it over and business boomed. The old factory is now completely gone and today they process many things—soups, puddings, Nescafé coffee—everything *but* the milk which now goes to Ault's factory in Winchester.

Story

During the Depression, village children brought their wagons to the coal yard where the fireman would throw on a shovel or two of coal for them to take home. There was no welfare and many townspeople kept from freezing with the bits of free coal thrown into the little wagons. Even the cinders were put to good use. Clarence Cross laughs about this:

The fine cinders discarded from the furnace were treasured by the farmers and other people for their driveway. It was understood that they could come and get the cinders every Monday. So there was a lot of competition among the farmers. It was decided that Monday began at Sunday midnight. So there would be wagons there waiting for the stroke of midnight to load up the cinders of which there was a limited supply. Then some started cheating. Their clocks would be out a half hour or so, so they'd be there at 11:30. So some that have very fine driveways today were those who couldn't tell what time it was.

On Queen Street you'll find the old brick Anglican Church. It has the only slate roof left in the village.

One of the liveliest places in Chesterville at the turn of the century was Flynn's Hotel on Main Street. The Flynns were great horsemen but they were a rough and ready crowd and their establishment attracted serious drinkers from miles around. Ignore the Sierra Grande sign that now hangs in front of this once-notorious drinking institution, and envision rows of horse stalls at the rear of the building with sounds of raucous laughter, fights, and quarrels coming from inside. The story is told of two young fellows who started a fight inside the hotel and came out to the stable yard to settle their differences. One fellow ended up dead, so one of the older men took the remaining lad to the train station, flagged down the midnight train, bought him a ticket for the west, and told him never to come back. He didn't. Another man was killed after being hit over the head with a whisky bottle, and to make it look like an accident someone threw the body into the stable under the horses' feet. The hotel still operates, but the old atmosphere was lost when the Flynn sign came down.

On Francis Street there is a building which is said to be constructed from the ruins of a sunken dredge. This is a typical example of a laborer's house built around 1900. The house was owned by Brodeur Bailey, an amateur vet who dehorned farmers' cattle, taking what was offered by way of payment. He kept a team of horses, a garden, a well, an outhouse, a cow, and some chickens—all on a 28 foot lot!

Elgin Froats kept pigs in a yard behind the little

house on the corner of Joseph and Francis Streets. Sometimes there would be as many as 100 pigs in the yard, not more than a stone's throw from Main Street. And no one had indoor plumbing!

Back on Main Street, and on your way out of the village, you will pass the site of the Kearns Block. Built at the turn of the century it housed stores, restaurants, a movie theater, and a dentist's office. Jerry Kearns and some friends went to Northern Ontario to search for gold around the time of the First World War. They struck pay dirt and named their claim the Chesterville Larder Lake Gold Mine. They couldn't raise enough money to develop it, so Jerry kept buying the shares from his partners. Finally in the 1930s he and his son managed to open the mine. He kept it going for many years until it was taken over by a conglomerate. In 1992 this fine old building was destroyed by fire, but memories of its namesake are very much alive.

As you leave Chesterville on Highway 43, notice the Hudson Allison home at the south edge of town on the east side of the road near the town sign. It's a big brick house now painted white with colored glass in the front windows. Hudson Allison was a local boy who went to Montreal, made money with insurance and stocks, returned, and bought this property in 1910. He erected these fancy buildings, imported horses and cattle, and employed many people. When he took his family on a trip to England a year or two later he decided to return on the ill-fated Titanic. Allison, his wife, and daughter went down with the ship but his son and the nursemaid were saved. The tragedy continued, however, when his son died young, without children. Several owners have run this farm. A man from South Africa, Lawrence Doering, worked it for years and it was known as the Doering Stock Farm, a lavishly run Jersey enterprise. A Dutch family who came to this country after the Second World War currently operates the farm.

R.R.

Winchester

Our next stop is Winchester, just a few kilometers west on Highway 43.

The first United Empire Loyalists settled along the banks of the St. Lawrence in Dundas County in June 1784. But the rear townships were not surveyed until 1798, so there was little settlement in these areas until the 1820s and 1830s. Bates Corner, the name originally given to Winchester after the first settler, a young Irishman, built a log cabin there, was settled in 1835. Initially supplies had to be obtained from Chesterville and mail was collected from Matilda (Iroquois). The village was renamed West Winchester when the first post office was established in 1855. It did not obtain its present name of Winchester until 1884, when the Canadian Pacific Railway built a line between Smiths Falls and Montreal which ran through the village.

The surrounding country was dense forest, and the production of squared timber for the Quebec market was one of the principal industries in the mid 1800s. A saw mill was constructed in the village by M.F. Beach in 1856; this was later expanded to include a grist and planing mill. By the 1870s the plant was one of the largest employers in the area, producing doors, sash-window-frames, and furniture.

It was at Winchester that famous dairyman John Ault bought a small cheese factory in 1923. From this humble beginning Ault Foods grew. It is said that "John had gone to an auction to buy a horse and ended up buying a cheese factory!" Whether this story is true, the fact remains that Ault Foods is one of the largest milk processors in Eastern Canada. The company owns 21 plants, 11 stores, has 2,200 employees, and sells $800 million worth of produce across the country. The Winchester plant produces butter, cream, and cheese and is the sole Canadian producer of demineralized whey, used in baby foods.

Winchester also has a process cheese plant owned by J.M. Schneiders, and the village holds an annual dairy festival in early August. Because of its long association with cheese production, Winchester likes to consider itself the "Cheese Capital of Ontario."

Quoted below is an abbreviated version of the Dairyman's Eleven Commandments. These Commandments were written in 1919 by Harlow M. Stiles, the editor of the *Official History of the Cornwall Cheese and Butter Board*:

1. Thou shall not abuse or worry thy cow—thou nor thy man-servant, nor they maid-servant nor thy dog, nor the mischievous boy who driveth her up; but thou shalt at all times treat her with

gentleness, and allow no one to molest her or make her afraid.
2. Thou shall not starve or stint thy cow for food, nor give her poor, innutritious, or unwholesome feed of any kind whatsoever . . .
3. The water that thy cow drinketh shall be pure water.
4. Thou shall give thy cows ample shade in the summer and a warm shelter in the winter.
5. When you milketh her, thou shalt lead her apart into a cool, quiet place, where there is naught to disturb her or make her afraid . . .
6. Thou shalt be clean, for lo! it standeth as an everlasting truth that cleanliness is next to godliness.
7. Thou shall cool and air thy milk as soon as drawn from the cow, by using the best appliances at thy command—not by putting cold water or ice into it.
8. Thou shalt not water thy milk.
9. Thou shalt not skim thy milk by taking off the cream that riseth in the can over night.
10. Thou shalt not commit adultery by adulterating thy milk with burnt sugar, chalk, salt, soda, or any ingredient.
11. Thou shalt love thy neighbor as thyself, and keep thy Sunday's milk at home for the use of thy family, and that the cheese-maker and all who labor with him in the factory may rest, and worship . . .

Surprising as it may seem Winchester, with its present population of approximately 2300, is still classified as a *village*. It was once mockingly described as "the Holy City" because it remained dry for a total of 76 years. Prohibition was not lifted until 1973.

Today Winchester is a modern village with its own Reeve and plenty of excellent facilities including a hospital, weekly newspaper, banks, library, arena, swimming-pool, ball-diamonds, numerous stores, and several restaurants. To make good its promise of rescinding prohibition, it even has a Liquor Store.

P.M.

Story

Many inhabitants of the United Counties are descendants of illustrious original settlers and early immigrants. This includes the offspring of two very important and prolific matriarchs of Dutch descent, Tidy Abberkerk and Aaltje Posch 4th. Both Tidy, who was born at Cassel, Ontario, and Aaltje, born in New York State but raised on an Ontario farm, were daughters of immigrant parents and went on to become the matriarchs of two of the most outstanding families in the country. The Posches and the Abberkerks became the foundation for the Rag Apple Line, the most predominant strain of Holstein cattle in Canada. And like other immigrant families that settled in this cold northern climate, they remain today because of their adaptability and hardiness.

The first Holsteins may have come to North America with Dutch settlers as early as 1621. Little evidence of these first imported animals remains, as

The perfect Holstein super cow. Introduced to Canada in 1881 by Michael Cook and Son of Aultsville, Holsteins laid the basis for the region's cheese industry. Illustration courtesy of Holstein Association of Canada.

they were probably allowed to cross with the dual-purpose cattle favored by the early farmer, who needed livestock capable of furnishing milk and beef. Serious breeding of the Holstein-Friesian did not begin until the mid-1800s after a New England farmer recognized the milk-producing capabilities of this cow.

In 1852 a Dutch ship loaded with rum docked in Boston harbor. Also onboard was the Holstein-Friesian cow that had produced copious amounts of fresh milk for the ship's crew on its long ocean crossing. She was sold to Winthrop W. Chenery of Belmont, Massachusetts, who was so impressed with her milk production that in 1857 he began importing stock from Holland. Records indicate that Chenery must have been an extremely dedicated and persistent breeder, for when a disease known as rinderpest hit his small herd and forced their destruction, he began again to import and develop a North American strain of Holstein-Friesian cattle.

Breeding in Canada began in 1881 when Michael Cook and Son of Aultsville (one of the lost villages under the St. Lawrence Seaway) bought one bull and nine cows from an American breeder. Within two years Herman Bollert of Cassel, Ontario had purchased foundation stock from Cook and it was here on Bollert farm that Tidy Abberkerk was born and Aaltje Posch 4th made her home. For 13 years Bollert raised fine Holstein cattle, but hard times forced him to disperse his herd in 1896. Bollert stock, however, continued to improve the herds of many Canadian breeders.

In 1924, using seed stock that originated on Bollert's farm, T.B. Macauly of Mount Victoria Farms in Quebec began breeding the animals that would come to be known across North America as the Rag Apple Line. The Holstein Association of Canada estimates that 95% of all dairy cattle in this country are either purebred Holsteins or those which clearly show Holstein characteristics. The majority of these animals can be traced to Bollert's two grand dames.

In just over a century Canadian breeding practices have produced world class stock that have been exported to 68 countries on every continent. It is the Dutch, however, and their more than 2,000 years of breeding history who are largely responsible for the development of this remarkable milker. Holland, with its rich green pastures and fine dairy herds, was famous even in the times of Caesar and Tacitus. The origins of these herds can be found with the Friesian and Batavian people who settled on the shores of the North Sea with their black and white Asiatic cattle. With slow and careful attention the Holstein-Friesian breed was developed and perfected into the super cow we see today.

Breeding practices and improvement of the breed have developed in the last 100 years probably more than in the last 2,000. With a better understanding of genetics and the introduction of artificial insemination and, most recently, embryo transfer, the Holstein breed continues to improve.

Not only has butter fat and milk production increased, but type—physical make-up—has also become an important breeding consideration.

Udders can be a problem for these queens of the dairy. Even the best milk producer is a liability to the farmer if a misshaped udder threatens to drag the barn floor, and in the modern milking parlor, with its highly mechanized milking machines, misplaced teats are a definite disadvantage. For the Canadian Holstein breeder this attention to detail was far more than 'udder' nonsense. In order to develop into a truly Canadian Holstein, these large animals require good feet and square legs strong enough to support them during their long winter months in the barn. Canadian breeders realized more than 60 years ago that a true production cow was a healthy, happy, long-living animal. The Canadian Holstein Association calls this Canadian cow, adaptable to our diverse climatic and geographical elements, a nearly perfect design.

This design began on the farm but soon moved to the laboratory, resulting first in the introduction of artificial insemination (AI) in the 1950s, and continues with today's embryo transfer programs.

What began more than 30 years ago as a futuristic, high-tech approach to herd improvement has become the norm for Canadian milk producers and serious breeders alike. Artificial insemination has not only made it possible for top bulls to produce more calves, but for the average farmer to bring better genetic strains to the herds using one, two, or more sires. Although not of primary concern, a decided advantage of AI has been the near elimination of the barnyard dairy bull, a temperamental, unpredictable and, at times, downright dangerous beast. The world of the Holstein has always been a matriarchy and AI has made it more so.

AI dramatically changed breeding practices all over the world in the dairy and beef business. The recent introduction of embryo transfer may be the next step in this quest for the designer cow. Embryo transfer (ET) makes it possible for a genetically superior cow to produce more calves in one year than she would in her whole lifetime using conventional breeding practices. One particularly prolific queen of the dairy is Werrcroft Model Doris, who has (so far) produced 89 et calves. Doris, it should be noted, has also produced 8 natural offspring making her what is known as a true producer, a cow capable of giving both an ample supply of milk and fine calves. It is cows like Doris who become candidates for ET.

Introduced in the 1970s and perfected in the 1980s, this method developed from an in-clinic surgical procedure to the simple, on-farm practice it is today. To simplify a somewhat detailed procedure, a top quality, proven cow is super-ovulated with hormone injections (to produce more than one egg) and artificially inseminated. The resulting embryos are removed and placed in cows who have good calving and mothering records.

A lot has changed since Tidy Abberkerk and Aaltje Posch 4th contentedly turned abundant Ontario grass and hay into sweet rich milk. Artificial insemination and the portability of frozen semen have made it possible for a bull long dead to sire calves in every corner of the world. New developments in micromanipulation such as cloning, sexing, and nuclear transplantation may one day also become common barnyard practices in the pursuit of the perfect designer cow.

One wonders just how good these animals can get. In the 1920s a select group of champion "Super

Cows" were producing annually more that 15,000 kilos of milk a year and over 500 kilos of butter fat. Today's Canadian "Super Cows" are showing tests of over 19,000 kilos of milk and more than 900 kilos of butterfat. But these are the patricians of the Holstein community, and not indicative of the animals found in most dairy barns. And it is the little guy who makes the difference, although the average Holstein, who produces 7,538 kilos of milk, 277 kilos of butterfat, and 240 kilos of protein, can hardly be called a little guy. It is these big hardy cows, who consistently produce for 12 to 14 years, that have shown the true production potential of this breed.

G.E.

Dundela

Our next stop is Dundela, home of the McIntosh apple. From Winchester, take Highway 31 south to Williamsburg, then take County Road 18 to Dundela.

American-born John McIntosh first homesteaded along the St. Lawrence River where it borders Dundas County in 1796. Five years later he married Hannah Doran, and moved inland to a crossroads that became known as McIntosh Corners (Dundela). Here he erected a log shanty in 1811. While clearing the brush to increase his quarter-acre of arable land, McIntosh found 20 apple trees which he transplanted to a garden next to his shanty. Using his humble dwelling for the settlement's first gospel meetings, and even as a school, McIntosh gradually improved

The original McIntosh Red Apple Tree and its discoverer Allen McIntosh, 1904. Courtesy S. D. & G. Historical Society, Inverarden Museum.

his farm, but failed to harvest any apples until only one tree remained in 1830. Tradition relates that fate now intervened, and a local farmhand taught one of McIntosh's sons, John, how to cut and graft trees—in this fashion John developed a tree which produced the first Mac.

Following custom, McIntosh named the fruit "Granny" in honor of his wife who nurtured the tree. His neighbors, thinking this was a common name for an uncommon apple, persuaded John to give it a distinctive label. He christened it the "McIntosh Red."

Despite the fruit's local popularity, John did not exploit it. However another son, Allen, did start a nursery with his brother Sandy. Allen became an itinerant preacher, and gave the seedlings out to everybody. Meanwhile his son Harvey Austin turned the nursery into a commercial enterprise and by 1876 was marketing the seedlings across the province. The Mac became popular province-wide in 1900 when Senator Smith of E.D. Smith and Sons of Winona came across it.

The Mac now left Canada to claim fame in the northern American states as "one of the most promising varieties of its class for general cultivation." It left North America when Dr. P.A. McIntosh of Spencerville shipped trees to Scotland, England, and Rhodesia.

All was not well for the original tree, though. Near tragedy struck in 1894 when the McIntosh house caught fire. The tree, only five meters away, was burned on one side. Badly damaged, it survived to bear fruit until 1906. To commemorate the tree's passing, local people took up a subscription to erect a monument. Remaining a small family orchard, the home and farm were sold at auction in 1974 after Samuel McIntosh died. McIntosh's widow simply said, "it's too much work for me." The *Ottawa Citizen* quoted her at the time as saying, "I was doing just about everything—spraying the orchards, being the hired man, even milking 16 cows a day sometimes." The last year's crop was lost due to an apple disease caused by insufficient spraying. Although various heritage organizations expressed interest in the farm, they backed off from buying it, citing "budget problems."

With two plaques in front of it, the old home is now a rooming house, and the orchard where "Every McIntosh . . . in the world originated," is overgrown. Fortunately from early July when picking starts, to September when the Mac is ready, the apple lives on to be enjoyed by everyone.

"The McIntosh: the apple Ontario gave the world" is still grown at Smyth's Orchards from 90 year old trees grafted just half a kilometer from the home of the first McIntosh apple. According to the present owner Paul Beckstead, Allen McIntosh's nurseryman, Samuel Smyth, "just started grafting a few of McIntosh's trees sometime before 1850, and never stopped." Today the family-run orchard boasts over 12,000 trees covering 100 acres of land, making it the largest in Eastern Ontario. In apple terms, that means Smyth's annually harvests some 1.8 million pounds of apples.

I.B.

Accommodations

Now that you've had your fill of cheddar and apple lore, you may want to rest over at the Country Farm Bed and Breakfast operated near Harrison's Corners by Vera Conroy. This rural B & B is located on the north side of Stormont County 18, one kilometer west of Harrison's Corners. R.R. #1, Lunenberg, Ontario K0C 1R0 (613) 534-2063.

Directions

To return home, retrace your route to Highway 31. Take the highway north to Ottawa, south to Cornwall and Highway 401. If you still long to know more about the history and culture of Eastern Ontario, read on. Some delightful armchair travels await you.

Armchair Traveling: A Guide to Further Reading

The Scot's love of learning means that books are held in high regard. This passion is often manifested at country auctions where local histories frequently fetch more than they would at nearby bookstores. This enthusiasm, coupled with a strong sense of their local heritage, guarantees that there is hardly a community in Stormont, Dundas, and Glengarry that cannot count at least one local history or author. This book list only provides some of the most significant works and is by no means complete. Most of these books and pamphlets may be found at public libraries, or for the rarer items at the Stormont, Dundas, and Glengarry Historical Society Archives kept at Inverarden Regency Cottage Museum. Unfortunately, with the exception of the general histories marked with an asterisk, they are not for circulation, but may be used for reference.

General Histories

If you academically inclined, you might as well start with Judge Jacob F. Pringle's *Lunenburg or the Old Eastern District.* (Cornwall: The Standard Printing House, 1890; rpt. Belleville, Mika Publishing).* The first history of the settlement of Eastern Ontario, this is still a standard work for anyone interested in genealogy. To find anything in this volume it is necessary, however, to obtain a copy of the index prepared by Lyall Manson from either the S.D. & G. Historical Society or the Sanctuary in Cornwall. This work was followed a half century later by John G. Harkness, *Stormont, Dundas and Glengarry: A History, 1784-1945* (printed by the United Counties of S.D. & G., 1946).* Covering the 20th century history of the United Counties with particular emphasis on politicians and the legal profession, Harkness leaves enough clues to allow the diligent to go beyond the facts alone. H. Belden and Company's *Illustrated Atlas of the Counties of Stormont, Dundas and Glengarry, Ontario* (Toronto: Belden & Co., 1879; rpt. Belleville: Mika Publishing)* is another in a series of Ontario atlases that provide written, cartographic, and illustrative accounts of the 19th century. Unfortunately though, if you weren't a subscriber you might not have been included, making it somewhat less useful than it could have been. An index has also been prepared for this work. The last and most comprehensive history of the United Counties was prepared by Frances and Clive Marin. Their *Stormont, Dundas and Glengarry 1945-1978*

(Belleville: Mika Publishing, 1982)* provides the most complete discussion of the upheaval caused by the Seaway in print and is an example of what local histories can aspire to be.

The standard work for Dundas County is J. Smyth Carter's *The Story of Dundas from 1784 to 1904* (Iroquois: St. Lawrence News Publishing House, 1905), still available at second-hand bookstores. The Glengarry mystique was lovingly explored by Royce MacGillivray and Ewan Ross in *A History of Glengarry* (Belleville: Mika Publishing, 1979).* My only lament is that the index is incomplete. Cornwall had to wait two centuries to have a comprehensive history produced. To celebrate the bicentennial, Elinor K. Senior's *From Royal Township to Industrial City, Cornwall 1784-1984* (La Bicentenaire de Cornwall Bicentennial Corporation, 1983)* was produced. Jam packed with facts and statistics, the book's best parts deal with the growth of Cornwall from a Loyalist outpost into an industrial center in the 1880s. Le Societe Historique de Cornwall at the same time produced an highly illustrative work where politics and facts merge in *Apercu de la Francophonie de Cornwall par l'image* (Societe Historique de Cornwall, 1984).* Finally for the military enthusiast there is William Boss' *Stormont, Dundas and Glengarry Highlanders, 1783-1951* (Ottawa: S.D. & G. Highlanders, 1952). This book is one of the best regimental histories available, thoroughly discussing the role of the Regiment from pioneer days through to the end of World War II.

Local and Personal Histories

Most villages, crossroads, hamlets, parishes, and many families have a printed history. Here is a list of some of the more general ones. Robert C.M. Grant, *The Story of Martintown: 1900-1940* (private printing, 1976),* provides an in depth glimpse of this old Glengarry village. It often sells for more at auction than at the booksellers. Eileen Merkely's substantive personal anecdotal history of *Cornwall The Friendly Town that Grew (a Reminiscence of Cornwall, Ontario)* (Cornwall: Union Publications, 1978)* is a must for nostalgia buffs. Leonard O'Dette's *Glimpses, Glances, Sideswipes of Dickinson Landing* (private printing, 1982)* is an idiosyncratic personal history of this "Lost Village." Eleanor W. Morgan's portrayal of Morrisburg in *Up the Front: A Story of Morrisburg* (private printing, 1964)* is an entertaining, fact filled research tool.

Neither have the small towns been left to enthusiasts. David M. Rayside's study of Alexandria, *A Small Town in Modern Times: Alexandria, Ontario* (Montreal and Kingston: McGill-Queen's Press, 1991)* tackles the notion of the idyllic small town and the Glengarry mystique head-on through a thorough examination of Alexandria, Glengarry's County town. If you or your family were ever from Lancaster and area, Ewan Ross' *Lancaster Township and Village* (private printing)* compiled in 1980 is a fascinating chronological listing of important events in the village and area history from 1790 to 1978.

Much of Stormont County is covered in a series of historical vignettes published in *Heritage Highlights of Cornwall Township* (St. Andrew's Historical Society

Bicentennial Committee, 1984).* This book is still available from the Cornwall Township Historical Society. In a similar vein the Williamsburg Women's Institute produced *Williamsburg Tweedsmuir Village History* (Belleville: Mika Publishing, 1984), a fascinating, well illustrated local history. Not to be outdone, L. Worral produced *Avonmore* (for the Avonmore Community Athletic Association, 1987), a carefully written examination of this rural Ontario community.

And finally ending with Glengarry, the pace was set by the Williamstown Bicentennial Research Committee in 1983 when they produced the illustrated *200 Years of Sharing 1784 Williamstown 1984*. The whole issue of the early Scottish migrations to Glengarry has been examined in a scholarly way in Marianne McLean's award winning *The People of Glengarry Highlanders in Transition, 1745-1820* (Montreal and Kingston: McGill-Queen's University Press, 1991).*

The Seaway

The Seaway project attracted significant editorial interest at the time, producing books that have become historical time capsules in themselves for their faith in "progress." A must in this genre is Lionel Chevrier's *The St. Lawrence Seaway* (Toronto: Macmillan, 1959);* as the Canadian politician most responsible for the building of the "canal," it is appropriate that "Mr. Seaway" be given the opportunity to tell his side of the story. Along the same lines Mabel T. Good's *Chevrier: Politician, Statesman, Diplomat and Entrepreneur of the St. Lawrence*

Seaway (Montreal: Stanké, 1987)* is a loving look at the career of Lionel Chevrier. This biography is also available in French. Carleton Mabee's *The Seaway Story* (New York: The MacMillan Co., 1961), however, notes with incredulity that while the engineers knew to the last bolt how many were used, no one knew how many human lives were affected by the Seaway, suggesting that progress was not completely unquestioned.

People

With numerous politicians and other assorted very important persons calling S.D. & G. their home, it should not be surprising that there are a number of biographies. Here is a short listing. Perhaps one of the most interesting local people was Dr. Locke, the "foot fixer" from Williamsburg. Certainly Rex Beach's *The Hands of Dr. Locke* (New York: Farran and Rinehart, 1932) was one of the most influential biographies towards confirming the good doctor's career. If you like political biographies, Bruce W. Hodgins' *John Sandfield Macdonald* (Toronto: University of Toronto Press, 1971)* will whet your appetite to learn more about Ontario's first premier. While Charles W. Humphries' *"Honest Enough to Be Bold," The Life and Times of Sir James Whitney* (Toronto: University of Toronto Press,1895)* provides enough detail for anyone who wants to understand the roots of political industrial Ontario. Finally Earle Thomas's *Sir John Johnson: Loyalist Baronet* (Toronto: Dundurn Press, 1986) provides a straightforward account of the man who led the Loyalists to Eastern Ontario.

Fiction

Much of the history and culture of Eastern Ontario is woven into historical fiction. As most of this fiction is now out of print and concerns Glengarry County, the best place to try to find these books is at Harriet MacKinnon's Glengarry Bookstore in Alexandria. Stocking the largest selection of contemporary local histories in the Counties, with a good selection of genealogical works, Harriet also carries out of print books by such authors as Ralph Connor and Grace Grant Campbell. Ralph Connor (C.W. Gordon), a Presbyterian and United Church Minister turned Glengarry novelist, is perhaps the most important perpetrator of the "Glengarry Mystique." Of his more than 30 works some of his most famous are *Glengarry School Days* (Toronto: Westminster Co. Ltd., 1902)*; *The Man From Glengarry* (Toronto: Westminister Co. Ltd., 1901)*; and *Torches Through the Bush* (Toronto: McClelland & Steward, 1934). Grace Grant Campbell is best remembered for *Thorn-Apple Tree* (New York: Duell, Sloan, and Pearce, 1943). Dorothy Dumbrille penned *Braggart in My Steps: More Stories of Glengarry* (Toronto: Ryerson Press, 1956); and *Up and Down the Glens: The Story of Glengarry* (Toronto: Ryerson Press, 1954). Perhaps the book most confused with fact is Carrie Holmes Macgillivray's *The Shadow of Tradition: A Tale of Old Glengarry* (Ottawa: Graphic Publishers, 1927).

Local Historical Societies and Heritage Groups

With seventeen different heritage groups, ten museums, and Upper Canada Village serving a population of about 100,000, it can safely be said that heritage preservation is alive and well in the United Counties. The following list highlights some of the leaders in this movement.

Cornwall Township Historical Society (St. Andrews West, Ontario, K0C 2A0). Along with holding regular meetings, the Society operates The Raisin River Heritage Centre in St. Andrews and a replica of the Old Log Church, circa 1784.

Glengarry Historical Society (P.O. Box 416, Alexandria, Ontario, K0C 1A0). The Society operates the Nor' Westers and Loyalist Museum in Williamstown, and the Glengarry Pioneer Museum in Dunvegan. It produces a regular newsletter, and an annual local history report called *Glengarry Life*.

Lost Villages Historical Society (P.O. Box 306, Ingleside, Ontario, K0C 1M0). The Society collects and preserves information about the Lost Villages. They have a display at the R.J. Saunders Energy Information Center (Hydro Power Dam) in Cornwall, and a small museum west of Cornwall's Guindon Park.

La Société franco-ontarienne d'histoire et de généalogie (La Regionale Saint-Laurent, C.P. 1894, Cornwall, Ontario, K6H 6N6). This society is connected with La Société historique de Cornwall.

Stormont, Dundas and Glengarry Genealogical Society (P.O. Box 1522, Cornwall, Ontario, K6H 5V5).

Stormont, Dundas and Glengarry Historical Society (P.O. Box 773, Cornwall, Ontario, K6H 5T5). This Society operates Inverarden Regency Cottage Museum and United Counties Museum, both in Cornwall. It produces eight newsletters a year, and holds regular meetings. The Society also has an extensive photographic archives collection at Inverarden Museum, and has published several books and pamphlets.

St. Lawrence Branch—United Empire Loyalist Association (P.O. Box 607, Morrisburg, Ontario, K0C 1X0).

Travel and Tourist Information Centers

Cornwall Chamber of Commerce,
132 2nd St. E., P.O. Box 338,
Cornwall, Ontario
K6H 5T1 (613) 933-4004

Cornwall Tourism and Convention Office,
340 Pitt St., P.O. Box 877,
Cornwall, Ontario
K6H 5T9 (613) 933-0074

Ministry of Natural Resources,
113 Amelia Street,
Cornwall, Ontario
K6H 5V7 (613) 933-1774
or 1-800-267-2401

Ontario Travel Information Centres,
903 Brookdale Ave.,
Cornwall, Ontario
K6J 4P3 (613) 933-2420
Highway 401 West,
Lancaster, Ontario
(613) 347-3498

St. Lawrence Parks Commission,
Morrisburg, Ontario
K0X 1X0 (613) 543-3704

United Counties of Stormont, Dundas and Glengarry, Economic Development,
594 St. Lawrence Street,
P.O. Box 364,
Winchester, Ontario
K0C 2K0 (613) 774-1234

INDEX

Alexandria 24, 33, 142-45
Apple Hill 131-32, 279
Aultsville 226, 229, 254-60, 297
Aultsville Station 206
Avonmore 273

Barnhart Island 227, 235
Berwick 273, 280
Bethune-Thompson House 95-97
Bout de l'Isle 78
Breadalbane 140-42
Brodie 140-42

Canada Mills 183-84
Cape Fear 14
Capitol Theater 174-75
Captain John McDonell's House 83-85
Carman House Museum 198-99
Caron House 86-87
Cassel 296, 298
Charlesville 26
Charlottenburgh Township 20, 31, 40, 61, 101
Chesterville 280-292
Chevrier Locks 158
Church of the Nativity 181-83

Cline House 178
Cooper's Marsh 31, 47-49
Courtauld's 184-85
Cornwall 12, 14, 16, 17, 20, 22, 24, 26, 27, 44, 62, 123, 142-43, 226, 227, 274
Cornwall Bridge 158
Cornwall Civic Complex 154-55
Cornwall District Courthouse and Gaol 166-69
Cornwall Grammar School 179
Cornwall Island (Grand Isle) 17
Cornwall Regional Art Gallery 169
Coteau 44
Crysler 280
Crysler's Farm 187, 211-12
Crysler Park 206

Dalcrombie 100-02
Dickinson's Landing 226, 231, 248-51
Dorion 73
Dundas Mill 183
Dundela 273, 302-05
Dulwich House 128-29
Dunvegan 139-40

Fairfield House 49-52
Farran's Point 189, 226, 229, 252-54
Fassifern 140-42
Finch 273, 280
First Baptist Church 178
Fort William 67, 71
Fraserfield 121
Fur Traders' Warehouse 73-78

Glen Nevis 140
Glen Roy 129-131
Grand Portage 71, 76, 77
Guindon Park 160-62, 241, 242

Harrison's Corners 305
Hoople's Creek 257-60

Ingleside 225, 227, 252, 275
Inverarden Regency Cottage Museum 31, 57-62, 185
Iroquois 187, 189, 193-201, 226, 227, 241
Ivy Hall 163-65

John Chesley's Inn 175-78

Kirkhill 140-42
Knox-St. Paul's United Church 178

Lac des Deux Montagnes 82, 83
Lac-Ste-Louise 80
Lachine 67, 73, 77
Lake St. Francis 40
Lakeview Park 242
Lamoureux Park 149, 154, 157

Lancaster 17, 18, 24, 29, 33-38, 115-16, 122
Lancaster Township 31, 116
Le Village 149, 152, 181-85
Limoges 276
Loch Garry 131
Lochiel 140-42
Lochinvar 140-42
Long Sault 227, 245-47
Long Sault Parkway 162
Longueuil 97

MacCrimmon 140-42
Manor House 89-90
Mariatown 201-02, 282
Marina 200 155
Martintown 101, 102, 122, 125-28
Massena 226, 227
Matilda Township 227
Mattawa 67
Mattice Park 184
Maxville 132-37
McQuaig's Corners 102, 121, 125
Mille Roches 189, 226-27, 231, 240-42
Monument Island 40
Moose Creek 273, 276
Morrisburg 26, 187, 189, 201-07, 227, 260-62
Moses-Saunders International Hydro-Electric Dam 158
Moulinette 189, 226, 231, 242-45
Mount Carmel 119

New Johnstown (Cornwall) 18

INDEX

Newington 275
Nor' Westers and Loyalist Museum 97-100

Old Author's Farm 225, 267-69
Osnabruck Township 20

Perth 278
Petite Isle 17
Pioneer Corner Craft Co-op 179
Pointe Fortune 67, 83
Pointe Maligne 14, 16, 18, 149
Prehistoric World 187, 209-211
Prescott 23
Priest's Mills 142

Riley's Bakery 171-73
Riverside Heights 207-09, 227
Roosevelt International Bridge 152
Rossi Artistic Glass 179
Route Panoramique 78-80

Salem Church 52-53
Sanctuary, The 170-71
Santa Cruz 251-52
Simon Fraser House 80-83
Skye 140-42
South Lancaster 29, 32, 38-44, 114
South Mountain 273
Squaw Island 40
St. Albert 276-77
St. Andrew's United Church 90-94, 128
St. Andrew's West 100, 102-08
St. Elmo 138-39
St. John's Presbyterian Church 179
St. Lawrence College 184
St. Mary's Catholic Church 87-89
St. Raphael's Church 118-20
St. Regis 14, 15, 18, 105
Ste-Anne-de-Bellevue 78-80
Stone House Point 53-57
Stormont Row Housing 175
Summerstown 49, 122
Sunken Townships 29, 32, 116-17

Trinity Anglican Church 175

United Counties Museum 179-81
Upper Canada Bird Sanctuary 187, 217-22, 255
Upper Canada Playhouse 225, 262-67
Upper Canada Village 187, 212-17, 227, 255, 276

Wales 226, 229, 247-48
Whitney Memorial Church 207-09
Williamsburg 271
Williamsburg Canals 189
Williamstown 45, 86-102, 121-23
Winchester 289, 292-95
Winchester Township 280
Woodlands 251-52

Printed in Canada